The Politics of Irish Freedom

This book is dedicated to the men, women and children who struggle for Irish freedom, and to freedom fighters everywhere.

THE POLITICS OF IRISH FREEDOM

GERRY ADAMS

BRANDON

First published in Ireland 1986
Brandon Book Publishers Ltd
Dingle, Co. Kerry.

First published in USA 1987
Brandon Book Publishers
27 South Main Street,
Wolfeboro, New Hampshire 03894-2069

© Gerry Adams 1986
Introduction © Steve MacDonogh 1986
Verses from 'The Rhythm of Time' reproduced by
permission of The Bobby Sands Trust.

Maps on pages 126 and 127 reproduced by
permission of *The Irish Nation*.

Contents

There's an inner thing in every man,
Do you know this thing my friend?
It has withstood the blows of a million years,
And will do so to the end.

It is found in every light of hope,
It knows no bounds nor space,
It has risen in red and black and white,
It is there in every race.

It lights the dark of this prison cell,
It thunders forth its might,
It is 'the undauntable thought', my friend,
That thought that says 'I'm right!'

From 'The Rhythm of Time'
Bobby Sands, H-Block, Long Kesh Prison Camp

Buíochas

THIS BOOK DOES not present itself as a definitive statement of present-day republican politics. Rather, it is a personal statement squeezed out, under the pressure of my publisher's coaxing, in whatever occasional fragments of free time I have been able to snatch in the last nine months. However, I hope it goes some way towards informing those people who are denied the opportunity to acquaint themselves with the general meaning, sense and motivation of modern republicanism.

I thank Steve MacDonogh for his perseverance. I would also like to thank Colette and Gearóid for their encouragement and patience, an Clann Mac Tomais for their hospitality, Tom Hartley for reading a first draft, Mary Hughes for her help with typing and Danny Morrison for reading the final draft.

Finally, I would like to thank the authors whose books and pamphlets influenced my writing; they will probably recognise themselves in the text; if not, and for other readers, a reference list is included.

Beir Bua,

Gerry Adams
October 1986, Belfast

Introduction

THIS BOOK IS neither an autobiography nor a statement of Sinn Féin's political programme. It is an expression by Gerry Adams of his politics. As President of Sinn Féin it falls to him to articulate party policy, but in this book he has set aside the narrow role of official spokesperson in order to be able to explore more widely and freely his politics as a republican.

He describes how he first became involved in politics in Sinn Féin and the West Belfast Housing Action Committee and in so doing he begins to elaborate in a practical and immediate way the politics of republicanism. He traces the changes that have occurred in the republican movement during the last twenty years and the issues that have been raised in the midst of the turmoil that has existed since 1968. While he does not seek to offer a history of the intervening years he does focus on certain key events and moments which have been crucial to the development of republican politics and strategy.

The notion of the book, which was suggested to him after the success of his earlier book, *Falls Memories* (Brandon, 1982), posed some problems for its author, particularly in terms of his position as 'leader'. In an objective sense he is a leader, as holder of the highest office in Sinn Féin and as his party's only Member of the British Parliament at Westminster. Observers and commentators credit him with having played the leading role in the development of republican policy and strategy in recent years. In the 26 counties one hears him spoken of as a leader in the traditional mould represented by Connolly, de Valera and Collins. Yet it is clear that he is not an exponent of traditional notions of leadership and that one of his most consistent concerns within Sinn Féin has been and remains the development of collective leadership.

In an article (*Iris* 10, July 1985) he recalled experiences in Long Kesh internment camp. Having developed his politics in the ad hoc circumstances of housing action and the youthful enthusiasm of the 1960s, he found the republican regime in the 'cages' very severe, 'to a degree which I for one found to be excessive.' Put in charge of a cage, 'we started a process of lectures, discussion and "crack". . . a whole process of co-education, of exchanging ideas and throwing things back and forth.' He sought to replace the kind of authoritarianism and instruction from superiors characteristic of any military organisation with a collective approach, and he offered in the same article the conclusion that 'leadership starts from the bottom and pushes upwards.'

In *Ireland After Britain* Ken Livingstone, then Leader of the Greater London Council, singled out the style of leadership in Sinn Féin for comment:

> If you sit and watch Gerry Adams in a group of people, he does not dominate it. He lets other people talk, he hears a consensus emerging, he doesn't try to provide charismatic dominating leadership. I've never been to a Sinn Féin *Árd Fheis* (conference), but others have expressed surprise at how everyone queued before the microphone, waiting to speak. What was remarkable, they said, was that when somebody had made the point that Gerry Adams wanted to make, he left the queue and returned to his seat. There are few male politicians who would behave in that way. The classic position of the Left in Britain is characterized by men who feel that no issue can be resolved until they have had their say.
>
> It seems to me that Adams and Morrison represent that alternative position which has a concept of a much more decentralized and more collective leadership. Part of it has to do with a perception of how much influence they have. If you have popular support, you don't need to shout that loudly; people will listen. It is also an awareness that things can't be achieved by individuals, and that is a lesson for us all.

The fact that Livingstone and others in the British Left feel a sense of kinship and solidarity with Sinn Féin has much to do with the developments of recent years in the republican movement with which Gerry Adams has been particularly associated. In the 1970s the movement was primarily involved in armed struggle; the conspiratorial methods which this emphasis required were confirmed by the traditional ethos of republicanism with its elevation of the suffering of the dedicated few and its conception of the Army Council of the IRA as the provisional government of the 32 counties.

For nearly fifty years after the 1916 Rising there was little development in the ideology of republicanism apart from the brief flowering of the Republican Congress in the 1930s. When Gerry Adams joined Sinn Féin in 1964 the movement was engaged in a process of critical reassessment under the leadership of Cathal Goulding in the wake of the failed IRA border campaign of the 1950s. But re-evaluation combined with the explosion of a situation of insurgency in the 6 counties led the movement to split in 1969/70; one wing, the 'Officials', embarked on a road which led them rapidly away from republicanism, while the other wing, the 'Provisionals', embarked on an almost exclusively military road. (Provisional) Sinn Féin was in the '70s a poorly organised support group of the IRA characterised by very a low level of internal discussion and debate.

The composition of the republican movement had in the process of the IRA's campaign of the '70s become decidedly young and working class, and the membership included many whose initial political involvement had been in the civil rights movement, in unemployed action groups and in housing action groups. Elements within the movement began to discuss what they saw as a lack of political development and by the late '70s they were beginning to advance alternative policies and strategies, to promote internal discussion and debate. The IRA had promised quick victory; it was becoming apparent, however, that victory was not around a corner and that more sophisticated methods and strategies were required for the long road ahead.

No instant change came over the republican movement. Undoubtedly, however, there was considerable internal jockeying for position which saw the emergence of a young, northern element in the leadership, replacing many of the older, more traditional and southern-based leaders. Behind these positional moves a debate was being conducted which re-examined Sinn Féin policies and strategies and promoted a more radical politics within the movement. Sinn Féin Árd Fheiseanna (national conferences) began to provide a forum which reflected real debate; the organisation's newspaper, *An Phoblacht/Republican News* developed from a rather ad hoc compilation of material to a centralised expression of party policy. Political activists began to be encouraged to plan interventions rather than being directed simply to sell newspapers and collect money for prisoners.

The planned development of new strategies was interrupted by the hunger strikes of 1980/81 but the changes that had taken place already within the movement undoubtedly made it more capable of leading a mass campaign in support of the hunger strikers' demands and more inclined to work with elements outside the movement. Cautious discussion of electoral strategy was dramatically cut across by the opportunity to stand Bobby Sands in the Fermanagh/South Tyrone election. The success in securing his election as Westminster MP constituted a massive popular endorsement of the hunger strike demands and, by extension, of the IRA. This support was copperfastened as at no other time in the history of the modern IRA as Bobby Sands and nine more hunger strikers died.

Reluctant to read the signs of the political development of Sinn Féin, newspaper commentators sought to explain the election of Sands and later of Owen Carron to the same seat and the electoral success of hunger strike candidates in the 26 counties as a temporary expression of humanitarian concern on the part of the voters. Thus media and politicians alike were again taken by surprise by the substantial electoral success of Sinn Féin from 1982 to 1986. Professional politicians watched aghast as Sinn Féin, whom they had been describing for years as political illiterates and gangsters surviving by intimidation alone, put together a whole series of electoral campaigns run by startlingly young activists who were unabashed by their lack of experience of the electoral game and who showed an energy and dedication to the task that made veterans of campaigns for established parties blink.

Gerry Adams, as President of Sinn Féin, represents a substantial political tendency. In Northern Ireland Sinn Féin has commanded in elections from 1982 to 1986 between 35% and 42.6% of the nationalist vote. Its military wing, the IRA, has maintained an armed struggle which has depended on an unquantifiable but significant degree of popular support from 1970 to the present. In the 26 counties Sinn Féin has not contested general elections in recent years but 41 Sinn Féin members have been elected to local councils. Some people will consider the publication of this book objectionable, but the simple answer is that Sinn Féin and the IRA exist and are important elements in Irish politics.

That there is a very widespread will to suppress the voice of radical republicanism is obvious. In the 26 counties all the major political parties have for many years supported the existence, renewal and implementation of Section 31 of the Broadcasting Act, the law by which members of Sinn Féin are prohibited from being interviewed on radio or television. In Britain and Northern Ireland television and radio stations do occasionally feature the expression of the republican position and interviews with Gerry Adams and other leading members of Sinn Féin have been broadcast. However, the structure of such programmes allows only for rudimentary and defensive elaboration of Sinn Féin's views on armed struggle; also, a large proportion of them (see Liz Curtis: *Ireland: the Propaganda War*) are censored, and such censorship is only the tip of the iceberg of invisible self-censorship by broadcasters. Newspapers and magazines report on Sinn Féin and IRA activities and very occasionally carry interviews with leading republicans, but such coverage is of its nature ephemeral and fragmentary.

There are those who would contend that because he is an unequivocal supporter of the armed struggle of the IRA Gerry Adams should be denied freedom of expression. Such reasoning is sometimes but not always employed cynically or dishonestly, nor is it always employed by people who are in a broader sense supporters of restricting freedom of expression. But it does always seem to be used selectively, and Section 31 in particular produces circumstances which make reportage of any integrity impossible. For example, when Owen Carron was elected as a Westminster MP it was his defeated opponent, Unionist politician and UDR officer Ken Maginnis, who was interviewed on RTE television news.

The involvement of Margaret Thatcher, Ronald Reagan and Mikhail Gorbachev not just in advocating but in executive responsibility for large-scale military action does not elicit suggestions that their freedom of expression should be curtailed. Such suggestions would, of course, be absurd, but when the objection to the voice of Gerry Adams is advanced as if it were based solely on his support for armed action, then a contradiction exists.

Another case in which the advocacy of armed struggle is used as the rationale for suppression is that of Nelson Mandela and the African National Congress (ANC). The Irish Anti-Apartheid Movement, however, of which Garrett FitzGerald was until quite recently a member, supports the right of the ANC to organise politically and militarily and has provided a platform for ANC speakers. Garret FitzGerald resigned from the movement, ironically enough not because of the movement's support for armed struggle and 'necklacing' suspected informers but because it allowed Sinn Féin to affiliate to it. Similarly, in Britain many elements of labour and liberal opinion that place Adams outside the bounds of political dialogue on account of his support for armed struggle nevertheless support the armed struggle in El Salvador and in South Africa and Namibia, expressing no reservations about the inevitable civilian casualties, and call for the unconditional release of Nelson Mandela. British Tory Minister Sir Geoffrey Howe meets with Oliver Tambo of the ANC. In recent years significant sections of the British Labour Party have recognised Sinn Féin as legitimate political representatives and have engaged in meetings and discussions with them. But clearly the relationship between political violence and freedom of expression is not a simple one and is characterised by considerable contradictions and confusions.

On the evidence, those who oppose freedom of expression for Sinn Féin do so not because of opposition to armed struggle in itself but because of disagreement with the pursuit of armed struggle in the particular circumstances of the 6 counties or because of disagreement with the aims and/or character of the IRA. However, in presenting, as they often do, their position as being simply 'anti-violence' they succeed in striking a resonant chord in many Irish people who are in general agreement with the politics of the republican movement and who even accept that the circumstances imposed by the British make violence inevitable, but do not wish consciously to countenance the death of a fellow human being. The Irish as a people have far more experience of being on the receiving end of violence than of dishing it out. Despite the establishment-sponsored glorification of the IRA of the War of Independence, the Civil War of only sixty-four years ago has left an indelible mark on the consciousness of a people who were never as dedicated to the organisation of military campaigns as almost all their European neighbours. Thus it is perhaps not surprising that there has been little pressure on the main political parties to end their support for and implementation of Section 31 of the Broadcasting Act.

The viewpoint that Sinn Féin should be as free to express its politics as any other party does not depend on agreement with Sinn Féin or the IRA. There are those who are resolutely opposed to the republican movement who would wish to see Sinn Féin members interviewed on television because they believe that Sinn Féin would thus be politically exposed and would lose support. There are also virulent opponents of republicanism in all its forms who would agree with the proposition, as Sartre put it, that 'freedom is indivisible', that one cannot abolish freedom of expression in one area without damaging freedom in all areas, that one cannot 'suspend democracy in order to save democracy', as was argued by the German government in the 1970s, or 'destroy the village in order to save the village', as was done by the US armed forces in Vietnam. That freedom is, indeed, indivisible is demonstrated by the pervasive atmosphere of censorship and self-censorship which extends like a cloak of mist from Section 31 of the Broadcasting Act.

The publication of this book will do nothing either to promote or to end violence. It may, however, promote and increase knowledge and understanding, and these are valuable commodities irrespective of any degree of sympathy or antipathy. Whatever one's opinion of it, the republican movement possesses a definable ideology, identifiable policies and a sense of political strategy, all of which are expressed by Gerry Adams.

Steve MacDonogh
Publisher

Political Origins

The development of democracy in Ireland has been
smothered by the Union.

James Connolly

IN 1961 THE last of the republicans interned during the
IRA's border campaign of the '50s were released. For most
of them it was a time for counting the cost and for adjusting
to life outside. There were no fanfares as they returned home:
imprisonment then, unlike today, evoked little active community
support or popularity; there were no coherent support organisations and the internees and their families were isolated.

I was thirteen years old and blissfully unaware of internment,
the IRA campaign and political matters in general. For me it
was a time of school exams — I had recently passed my 'Eleven
Plus' — of hurling matches and long summer holidays. My father
had just returned from working in England and he and my
mother were contemplating emigrating to Australia; uncles and
aunts were already scattered in Canada, Dublin and England.

A few of the released internees set about picking up the pieces
of a scattered and demoralised organisation; in 1961 the total
strength of the Belfast IRA was 24, their total armaments were
two short-arms. Republicanism had not died but it had suffered
a substantial defeat and amongst those who remained active a
process of reassessment was begun while a low level of political
organisation commenced.

Wolfe Tone committees were established by republicans
throughout Ireland to mark the 200th anniversary in June 1963
of Tone's birth. Theobald Wolfe Tone, the founder of Irish
republicanism, was a Protestant barrister who, influenced by
the American and French revolutions, set up the Society of
United Irishmen in 1791 to unite 'Protestant, Catholic and
dissenter' in the cause of Irish independence, and was secretary
to the Catholic Committee which campaigned for civil rights for
Catholics. He attempted to gain French military support for the

fight for independence but was captured in 1798 and sentenced to death; he cheated his captors by killing himself before the sentence could be carried out.

At the commemoration in Belfast an internal controversy provoked a local leadership crisis in the republican movement. It was the practice of republicans to carry the Irish tricolour on parades, despite the fact that the flag, as the symbol of Irish nationalism, was banned under the Flags and Emblems Act (1954). The failure to carry it in June 1963 in defiance of the ban sparked off a period of infighting at the end of which a Belfast leadership supportive of Cathal Goulding, Chief of Staff of the IRA since the previous year, was firmly in control.

The tricolour played a role too in bringing me into politics. During the Westminster elections in October 1964 rioting occurred after a tricolour was displayed in the window of Sinn Féin's election office in Divis Street in Belfast. Ian Paisley objected loudly to the display of the flag and threatened to march on Divis Street and remove it within two days if it hadn't been removed by then. The next day a force of RUC men broke down the door of the office and removed the flag. Two days of intense rioting followed and the republicans, accompanied by a large crowd of local people, replaced the flag, only to have it removed again by RUC men wielding pick-axes. Three hundred and fifty RUC men using armoured cars and water-cannon and wearing military helmets launched an attack on the Falls and 50 civilians and 21 RUC ended up in hospital. The government had responded to pressures from Paisley and had provoked a violent reaction from the Catholic working class. It was a stark reminder of where the balance of power lay in the 6 counties.

I was in school at the time but the Divis Street events concentrated my mind on politics. I already possessed a vague sense of discontent and the naked display of state violence against the people of the Falls made me feel I did not want merely to stand by looking on. I found myself spending a few evenings in the Felons Association rooms on the Falls Road folding election material for Liam McMillan, the Sinn Féin candidate. Despite, or maybe because of, all the republican candidates losing their election deposits, within a few months I joined Sinn Féin.

I suppose I was a member for about 18 months before I realised what I was in at all; I had, after all, joined as a reaction to what had happened in Divis Street. This had had the effect of reawakening a sense of national consciousness which whetted my political appetite. I was eager to find out why things were as they were and as I read those history books which were not on our school curriculum I became increasingly aware of the nature of the relationship between Ireland and Britain. Having reached the conclusion that this relationship was a colonial one and having decided that it must be ended I began with youthful innocence the task of ending it. My new-found knowledge dictated the logic that the British government had no right to govern any part of Ireland, that that right belonged to the Irish people and that we could surely govern ourselves in our own interests more efficiently than anyone else. All we had to do was to get rid of the British. With that I was, I felt, starting off on the right foot. I was to discover that I was a long way from fully understanding how we might get there.

I had a republican family background. My maternal grandfather, a prominent full-time trade union organiser on personal terms with both James Connolly and James Larkin, had worked for de Valera in the 1918 election; my paternal grandfather and his in-laws traced their republican involvement back to the Irish Republican Brotherhood (IRB). They reared republican sons and daughters who included my mother and my father who was shot and wounded by the RUC and imprisoned in the 1940s. In spite of all this I was no more politically conscious than many of my contemporaries, but the everyday aspects of our situation were obvious enough: bad housing, poverty, political structures with which we could not identify and, above all, the endemic, structural unemployment. Many of my contemporaries left, complaining that the sectarian state where everything was rigged against them from the start was no place for a decent life; others reckoned they would stick it out and see if maybe they couldn't bring about some improvements.

I decided to stick it out. I was never in any doubt that I would. I loved the city of Belfast, its streets, its hills, its people; it was the world I knew and I had no intention of being forced out of my own place. I was also naive, like most of my generation, and thought that a few rational, sensible changes could easily be made which would improve the quality of life and bring about equal opportunities for all.

That sense of possibility was what lay behind my decision to become involved in political activism. The options were clear: you could emigrate; you could stay and adopt an attitude of passivity which would hopefully get you by; or you could get involved in trying to change things. Of course, I had absolutely no idea then of where this would lead me or of how events in the 6 counties would develop; none of us did. We were certain only of one thing: the injustice of the system could not go unchallenged. It was wrong. Irish national self-determination was the only solution.

Sinn Féin was a very small organisation then. It was also illegal. You could almost describe it as an incestuous association, made up as it was of members of a few spinal republican families, some of whom could trace their involvement right back through the '50s, '40s, '30s and '20s to the Fenians and the Irish Republican Brotherhood (IRB) and perhaps even beyond. There was a small number of young people — mostly from republican backgrounds like myself — a larger number of much older people, and a middle group of people who had been active in the 1950s; that is, people who had been imprisoned then.

The mid-'60s was a period of turmoil in the republican movement. Following the failure of the '50s campaign there was a major rethink. The impetus for debate came from the leadership but the need for reassessment was naturally apparent in the organisation as a whole. In Belfast we were picking up an outer ripple of a wave which was centred at national leadership level in Dublin. Accordingly several developments were taking place more or less simultaneously both inside and outside the movement.

The Wolfe Tone Societies, formed in 1963, had become a meeting point for republicans and socialists, for Irish language enthusiasts and communists. They held occasional seminars and while little actual work was done the societies in Dublin, Cork and Belfast provided a platform for ideas and an important gathering point for anti-imperialist opinion makers.

This was set against a political background in the 6 counties which was characterised, on the nationalist side, by low-level social justice campaigning by individuals and small groups, most notably the Dungannon-based Campaign for Social Justice. The Dungannon people documented instances of discrimination and briefed the London-based Connolly Association, its *Irish Democrat* newspaper and a minority element in the British Labour Party, based around Kevin McNamara MP.

Despite this the Unionists ran the 6 county state exactly as they wished. And as long as British interests were safeguarded there was no British interference. Apart from some of the more obvious features, 'Northern Ireland' was a police state similar to South Africa's apartheid system. It was a one-party state, 'a Protestant parliament for a Protestant people'. Efforts to change this by physical force activity, by publicising the injustices or by the development of a party political alternative had failed. There were none of the usual manifestations of normal class politics; partition and sectarianism ensured that this was the case. Indeed I came into politics just as the Northern Ireland Labour Party (NILP), which had enjoyed some popularity with electoral gains in 1958 and 1962, was poised to commit political suicide on the issue of whether swings in public parks should be chained up on Sundays.

Nationalist opinion was represented by the conservative Nationalist Party though in Belfast and Derry there were more radical tendencies which were to come to the surface again in the years ahead. The Nationalist Party was occasionally abstentionist, totally ineffectual and politically amateur. It did not satisfy the needs of the emerging, better-educated, Catholic middle class, a section of whom were committed to working for social and economic reforms within the 6 county state. After some attempts to ginger-up and democratise the Nationalist Party through a National Unity association which was established by a group of Catholic graduates, the rival National Democratic Party was formed. This development and Dublin premier Sean Lemass's acceptance of an invitation by Terence O'Neill, the new Prime Minister, to visit him at Stormont led to the Nationalist Party entering the Stormont parliament and becoming the official opposition.

The Lemass/O'Neill meeting was probably the first step by Fianna Fáil towards recognising the 6 county state. It flowed naturally from the North/South collaboration against the 1950s IRA campaign. This, together with the acceptance by the Nationalist Party of the institutions of the state and the emergence of a politicised Catholic middle class in the National Democratic

Party, pointed the direction for the possible rehabilitation of the 6 counties. Those who sought such a reformation took succour from O'Neill's apparent willingness to apply to the state the democratic veneer necessary for the demands of the twentieth century. But even at that stage it was too little too late. 'No Surrender' Unionism would not be so easily brought to heel and already in the opposite camp, within the radical anti-Unionist ranks, the disparate ingredients involved in the slow fermentation of agitational activity were coming together.

In 1965 the first Republican Club was set up in Belfast in an effort to break the ban on Sinn Féin. In the same year republicans attempted to set up 'One Man, One Vote' Committees. However, largely because of their lack of political acumen, allied to the hostility of the NILP, that initiative floundered, but only temporarily. Within the Wolfe Tone Societies, the question of civil rights in the 6 counties had become a recurring theme. In August 1966 they hosted a conference on civil rights in Maghera, County Derry and another in November in Belfast where republicans were enjoying a rise in local support. In 1963 they had been badly fragmented over the question of whether to carry the tricolour or not, in 1964 the flag was seized and rioting resulted, but in 1966 West Belfast saw a massive display of tricolours and banners in the parade to celebrate the 50th anniversary of the Easter Rising.

This Easter commemoration received very widespread support from nationalists and involved cultural associations, trade unionists and social groups: there were organisations, almost street committees, for the making of flags, buntings and banners. There was a one-day pageant at Casement Park in Andersonstown and a week of events including concerts and the like, and for the parade itself about 20,000 people turned out.

In the Unionist press there were scare stories about the IRA and the 'B' Specials were put on stand-by. Two or three Belfast republicans received prison sentences for organising the parade, which was illegal, and in Newry a local republican was charged under the Flags and Emblems Act. At this time also a major influence in moulding the political character of my generation of republicans was the popularisation of the writings of the leaders of the 1916 Rising, in particular the writings of James Connolly. The process of political education within the republican ranks was enhanced by the availability of a flood of publications and we began to develop a view of the class nature of the struggle and of the relationship between its social and national dimensions.

The slight raising of the political temperature at this time led to a number of small but dangerous developments. In the months before Easter there were petrol bomb attacks on Catholic homes, shops and schools. In May a Protestant woman died in a petrol bomb attack on the Catholic-owned public house next door to her home.

The following month Paisley led a demonstration against the General Assembly of the Presbyterian Church. What is sometimes forgotten is that he marched to that demonstration through Cromac Square, a Catholic area. The residents who attempted to block the road were very brutally dispersed by the RUC who returned the following night and renewed the assault. The IRA played a small part in organising people against these RUC incursions and one local republican activist received a prison sentence. A few weeks later Peter Ward was killed and two other Catholics were wounded outside the Malvern Arms public house on the Shankill Road. On the same night a loyalist gang had attempted to enter the home of Leo Martin, a prominent republican. It was also discovered that a Catholic man, John Scullion, who died on 11 June, had been shot on 27 May in Clonard Street by a loyalist terror gang. On 23 July Paisleyite marchers rioted in Belfast city centre, attacking the Catholic-owned International Hotel and attempting to burn down a bookmaker's in Sandy Row which employed Catholics.

These incidents offered examples of the politico-religious relationship within loyalism. The crisis of loyalism, as always, was finding its expression in attacks on Catholic property and in the assassination of Catholic people. At the trial of three UVF members for the murder of Peter Ward the RUC stated that Hugh McClean, one of the defendants, had said when charged, 'I am terribly sorry I ever heard of that man Paisley or decided to follow him'.

In the midst of the growing tensions, republicans were trying to come to terms with the needs of the struggle, the needs of the people and the relevance of the struggle to the people and to the Ireland of the 1960s. There have always been three tendencies within the republican movement: a militaristic and fairly apolitical tendency, a revolutionary tendency, and a constitutional tendency. Throughout the history of the movement one or other of these has been in the ascendancy. Since partition, however, there had been no dominant tendency capable of giving proper and relevant leadership to the mass of Irish people.

By the mid-'60s the movement had shed most of its militaristic leanings and a small, politically conscious organisation was developing and beginning to examine critically the role of republicanism and the task of finding a strategy towards the goal of an independent republic.

As part of a major review of strategy the whole relationship between revolutionary struggle, armed struggle and mobilisation of the masses — all of those now tired jargon phrases — was discussed at length. A very thorough and useful analysis was presented, which went right back to the days of agrarian struggle and the Fenians. Various questions were examined in a historical sense: why, for example, had Fintan Lalor failed, why had the Fenians failed, and so on. The republican movement had long been a conspiratorial movement which manifested itself almost exclusively in physical force actions. Since Connolly, Pearse and Mellows and the Republican Congress of the 1930s there had been no real effort to put any meat on the ideas of what type of a republic was aimed at.

The impact of this major review was that Sinn Féin began to define its politics more, to the extent of talking about a 'workers' republic', 'a worker's and small farmers' republic' and a 'socialist republic' or a 'democratic socialist republic'. But what came most clearly from these discussions was a recognition that republicans needed to identify their philosophy as being relevant not to the vision of a future Ireland but to the actual Ireland of today, and that they needed to enlist mass support, or at least the maximum support possible, for the republican cause. As we immersed ourselves in the business of political education that truth became of paramount importance. We could not free the Irish people. We could only, with their support, create conditions in which they would free themselves.

These kinds of conclusions resulted in people like myself becoming involved in housing action and the other agitational activities which the movement had begun to promote. In the 26 counties republicans became involved in the Waters Restoration Committee, a campaign for the restoration of inland waters to the Irish people. There were campaigns against absentee landlordism and against foreign investors; in one case at least this took the form of military action. An IRA volunteer from Cork was killed and Cathal Goulding was tried for incitement over his speech at the funeral.

There was a realisation that one could not organise politically as an illegal organisation; the party newspaper could not be sold, the Special Powers Act could be used against the organisation and its members at the whim of an RUC inspector, and so on. So, that led to making a priority of the attempt to fight the ban on Sinn Féin and this was a conscious decision to leave the back-room conspiracies and come out into the open.

The IRA in Belfast occasionally came into public prominence itself. Towards the end of 1966 a British army recruiting class at St Gabriel's School was broken up by volunteers armed with hurling sticks and in 1967 there were three attacks on British Army training centres — two in Belfast and one in Lisburn. By this time there were five Republican Clubs in Belfast and I had graduated to being the PRO of the Andersonstown one. Contrary to its title our small membership covered Ballymurphy, Turf Lodge and part of the Falls as well.

Our relatively low-level agitation in Belfast, the rising political temperature and the new openness of the republicans was bringing us into contact with various elements: members of the Communist Party, the NILP, the Republican Labour Party, Young Socialists and people who had long records of working against discrimination. We were meeting through the Wolfe Tone Society, through debates in St Malachy's Old Boys' Club, and through the beginning of the revival of Irish music. The sessions and fleadhs provided gathering points — in the docks, in the city centre, in the Falls — and over a pint people who might otherwise not have met were discussing the politics of the day. I worked in a pub, the Duke of York, at that time; it was close to the head office of the NILP and a number of trade union offices, as well as the *Newsletter,* and there you got a mingling of NILP and CP members, republicans, trade union officials and journalists discussing issues of the day.

The Vietnam war was one of those issues and I was one of many who went along to rallies against the war. Similarly, the black civil rights campaign in the United States not only had its obvious influence in terms of the anthem of 'We Shall Overcome' but also in terms of its affinity with what was happening in the 6 counties. Courtesy of television we were able to see an example of the fact that you didn't just have to take it, you could fight back.

People did not live their lives in isolation from the changes going on in the world outside. They identified to a greater or lesser extent with the music, the politics, the whole undefined movement of ideas and changes of style. Bob Dylan, the Beatles and the Rolling Stones, long hair and beads, the 'alternative society', music and fashion were all markers put down by a new generation against the complacencies of the previous one, and one of the most important messages to come across was that one *could* change the world. This was the promise of the '60s, that the world was changing anyway and the tide of change was with the young generation. This produced a sense of impatience with the status quo allied to a young, enthusiastic and euphoric confidence.

The public declaration of their existence by the Republican Clubs brought this mingling of elements into a new focus, and a deal of attention became centred on the demand for the lifting of the ban, which had been slapped on them almost immediately. There was a meeting in Chapel Lane at which republicans demanded that they be recognised and Liam Mulholland announced publicly that he was the Chairman of the 6 County Executive of the Republican Clubs. Next day a newspaper had a huge photo of Liam and the headline: THIS MAN IS HEAD OF AN ILLEGAL ORGANISATION. When the Republican Clubs were banned students at Queen's University immediately announced themselves as a Republican Club and from this small start young radicals like Michael Farrell, Tom McGurk, Bowes Egan and others came into a certain prominence and also came into contact with other political influences. Shortly after this a colleague and myself were arrested for selling the *United Irishman* in what was a planned defiance of the ban on that newspaper. We were released, however, without being charged. While we were thus robbed of the opportunity of fighting a political case in the courts, one of the pickets who had retired patiently to a nearby pub while waiting for our arrest was so incensed and inebriated when the RUC eventually frogmarched us to the barracks that he found himself, contrary to instructions, attacking the arresting party and getting heavily assaulted and subsequently fined. We, of course, had to organise a collection to defray his court costs and pay the fine.

In Derry, Eamonn McCann (of the Derry Labour Party) and Finbar O'Doherty (of the local Republican Club) and others were busy exposing and opposing the appalling housing situation arising from the specific forms of discrimination there. In Dublin, Cork and Waterford Housing Action Committees were also active and occasionally a number of us would travel to Dublin to attend housing marches and protests. The success of these activities led a few of us in Belfast to get together on the same issue and we set up the West Belfast Housing Action Committee.

An example of the kind of activity we became involved in was a case when I was approached by people called Sherlock who were living off the Falls Road in Mary Street, which was a very small street of two-bedroomed houses in very bad condition indeed. We brought them along to the Housing Trust and tried to get them rehoused, and when no movement was forthcoming we simply took over a flat in what was then the beginning of the Divis Flats complex. In Derry and in Caledon similar squats had already taken place with some success. The Caledon instance, which had been organised by the local Republican Club, had received considerable media attention when Austin Currie, then a Nationalist MP, became involved.

The Sherlock case was the first instance in Belfast; it received some media attention and was successful in the end because the family was allocated a new house. And that experience and success provided us with a major impetus: it was proof that direct action could work and it was something that enjoyed popular support in the area. After the years and years of atrocious housing, here, at last, some break seemed to have been made. The Housing Action Committee was a very ad hoc creation, called into existence on the second day of the occupation. From this start we embarked on a campaign of occupying and picketing the Housing Trust's offices, and we found that other people came to us looking for help. Earlier we had attempted to agitate against the building of the Divis Flats complex, but without evoking popular support. Now we found we were able to organise in a much more coherent way with much more support, and the residents of the Loney district marched against the tower blocks and in favour of the rebuilding of their own traditional houses.

There were only six or seven of us from the movement involved in the housing agitation and in the unemployment agitation which also developed but when the Northern Ireland Civil Rights Association (NICRA) was formed following an initiative by the Belfast Wolfe Tone Society with the assistance of the Campaign for Social Justice, the small groups active around such issues fitted naturally into the wider civil rights struggle. The meeting to establish NICRA was well attended and was packed by republicans, who wielded the biggest bloc vote.

Contrary to later claims by the Unionists that republicans took over the civil rights movement, we were there from the very beginning. Republicans were actually central to the formation of NICRA and far from using it as a front organisation those of us who attended the inaugural meeting were directed to elect only two of our membership to the executive. NICRA went through a low-key period of citizen advice activity at first. It held protest rallies in Newry and Armagh in 1968 after the banning of an Easter Commemoration parade in Armagh but it turned down a republican proposal for a Belfast march.

The first NICRA march took place in August 1968 from Coalisland to Dungannon. It was barred from the centre of the town, a rally was held in front of an RUC blockade and the crowd dispersed following some confusion between the republicans and the others as to whether they should sing the Irish national anthem or the American black civil rights anthem. It was unimportant. The civil rights struggle had begun and the Coalisland-Dungannon march was the beginning of a broad-based, if uneasy and sporadic alliance between all the anti-Unionist elements in the 6 counties. October 5 in Derry was to accelerate the process.

The organisers of this Derry march sought sponsorship from NICRA and from prominent people in the local community, including John Hume, who refused. NICRA very reluctantly and belatedly endorsed the march and Stormont banned it; the scene was set for confrontation. The republicans decided that if there was going to be trouble the people who should get hit should be the visiting MPs who had been invited to attend as observers. As the late Liam McMillan recalled in a pamphlet:

The Belfast republicans had been instructed in the event of the parade being halted by police cordons to push leading nationalist politicians or any other dignatories who were sure to be at the head of the parade into police ranks. This they did to such effect that one became the first casualty of the day of violence, receiving a busted head. In the ensuing clash the RUC spared no-one. A British MP, Mrs Anne Kerr, who had been invited over as an observer said the savagery that day was worse than anything else she had seen during the Chicago riots a short time previously. And the television coverage of the RUC brutality exposed the fascist nature of the Orange-Unionist domination and its ruthless denial of elementary democratic rights to a large section of its citizens.

A sizeable Belfast contingent went to the march. Unable to get yet another day off work I watched the TV coverage of the RUC smashing into the demonstrators who were only a few hundred strong. The following week a protest march against RUC brutality drew 15,000 people and NICRA felt confident enough to state its demands clearly: universal franchise in local elections, an end to gerrymandered boundaries, the repeal of the Special Powers Act, an end to housing discrimination, disbandment of the 'B' Specials and the withdrawal of the Public Order Bill which the Unionists were pushing through Stormont to outlaw civil rights demonstrations.

These demands also became a focus for the emerging differences between the republican leadership and some rank and file activists. The leadership felt that a democratisation of the 6 county statelet was necessary if republicans were to engage freely and legally in the social and economic struggle which affected both the Unionist and anti-Unionist working class. From involvement in these struggles would emerge, they argued, a united republican working class. For them the civil rights struggle was therefore a serious attempt to democratise the state. In the process the national question would be subordinated in order to allay Unionist fears and because the democratisation was going to be a lengthy one, the movement was to be demilitarised. This theory had one serious defect: it underestimated the reactionary nature of the state itself and the reluctance of the Westminster government and its management at Stormont to introduce reforms.

The contrary position was dawning slowly upon those of us who were deeply involved in grassroots agitation. We were beginning to realise that the 6 county statelet could not be reformed, that by its very nature it was irreformable and that the major effects of the civil rights struggle would be to show clearly the contradictions within the state, its colonial nature and the responsiblity of the British government for this situation. This position only became clear as the civil rights struggle and the state's backlash intensified and as the leadership's position clarified.

The leadership maintained that following the democratisation of the state there could be a coming together of Protestant and Catholic workers in support of progressive politics, and the way to achieve this was through a heavy involvement of republicans in the trade unions. Having accepted the desirability of finding common, neutral ground on which Catholic and Protestant could combine, the trade union movement was, on the British Communist Party model, identified as the organisation in which we should be involved and which provided that mutual ground.

The strategy flew in the face of James Connolly's analysis of the loyalist workers as 'the aristocracy of labour'. It also flew in the face of reality, not least the reality of Catholic working class employment and unemployment. The members of the republican movement in the 6 counties who were supposed to implement this strategy were mostly Catholics who, if they had jobs had mostly unskilled ones, and who had little or no meaningful access to trade unions. The vast majority of members were either unemployed or were building workers; there were no professional people involved at all, and the few skilled workers were bricklayers and joiners on building sites, occupations with a notoriously low level of union organisation. With a ready labour market there was little motivation or opportunity to organise successfully.

Members of the Dublin leadership of the republican movement came to Belfast and I was among those who went to the lectures they gave. I found them very interesting and instructive but they failed to accord with my experience and opinions at that time. In my view, and to some degree with hindsight, the development of the 'stages' theory of progressive democratisation was conditional in the first place on the state and its supporters being willing to redress the state's own injustices. This, it was rapidly becoming apparent, was hardly the case. In particular I felt that the analysis of the ways to unite the Protestant and Catholic working class ignored the very nature of the state and my own occasional personalised and parochial encounters with loyalism.

Where I lived in Ballymurphy the relationship between Protestant and Catholic was devoid of any sectarian difficulties. Neighbouring Moyard and New Barnsley were Protestant estates and there was a good level of social intercourse between people of my age. A crowd of us used to go regularly to Moyard and meet with young people there. We would hang around the corners, talk and take our chances with the local talent. We never discussed politics or religion except in a joking or bantering fashion. Then I became involved in a small campaign which involved both Catholics and Protestants.

On the Springfield Road a child from New Barnsley had been knocked down at the junction with the Whiterock Road and I went to New Barnsley and saw the parents and then went to Ballymurphy which even in those days had a fairly energetic and well organised tenants association. We organised a small campaign to have safety rails put up at the corner and also to have a pedestrian crossing nearby. The campaign was successful and we were delighted. Not only was it a gain, albeit small, but it was Catholics and Protestants coming together — in a very parochial sense but nonetheless coming together — and agitating. News of this percolated upwards into the Unionist establishment and one of Paisley's people arrived on the scene and for the first time I heard serious talk about 'papists' and 'pope-heads' and 'fenians' and 'taigs'. The Protestants in New Barnsley who had previously been involved with us just stopped their involvement like that.

What we were saying to the Dublin visitors was, 'Look, you can talk about all this coming together of Protestant and Catholic working class but here's yet another instance where the sectarian card was played and the people who had been united were effectively separated. Your notions just don't square with reality.' If the state would not allow Catholics and Protestants to get a pedestrian crossing built together, it would hardly sit back and watch them organise the revolution together.

They also saw the trade unions as a main means of pursuing

politics. But again my experience gave me doubts. I was working as a barman and was sacked for demanding the trade union rate for the Twelfth of July holiday, which was double time and a day off in lieu. I went to the trade union of which I was a member and wanted them to fight it but they wouldn't. Although there were no sectarian overtones it was characteristic of the fact that apprentices were a dime a dozen and in this context even when one tried to look for something very simple through the trade unions they just didn't respond.

My own experience was that the sectarian card could be invoked effectively and that there was little basis for making any progress on the national question through the trade union movement. And both of these experiences flew in the face of what the republican leadership was proposing.

The nature of the civil rights struggle added to these contradictions. For example, the directive to Belfast republicans to push visiting notables into the front line at Duke Street on 5 October in Derry was really a commonsense instruction. But it also accepted that while attempting to democratise the state there was a need for dramatic confrontations in order to expose what was wrong. And these confrontations flatly contradicted the leadership's position of being non-provocative. Furthermore, the people who were making the running on the ground were developing their own thinking on the issues which confronted us. We were not at the centre of the policy making process but we were in the centre of what was happening on the ground so that, for example, in January 1969, following the loyalist and RUC attacks on the Burntollet marchers it was republican stewards who took the initiative, discarded their armbands, and turned with gusto on the RUC at a banned march in Newry.

The other important development was of course the emergence of People's Democracy after the 5 October march. They were to have the most unified approach of all the elements involved in the civil rights campaign. It was they by their Burntollet march in January '69 who showed that the reforms promised by O'Neill in November '68 and the public relations exercise which followed his 'Ulster at the Crossroads' television appeal in December of that year were meaningless.

The Burntollet march showed that nothing had changed. The British state of Northern Ireland had certainly not made reforms gratuitously. It would never of its own accord have even moved towards a situation of doing away with some of the things which were disfiguring the state. In fact these things were quite consciously maintained and once there was any movement towards removing them the very foundations of the state became insecure. In hindsight it was inevitable, as we approached 1969, that we were headed for a major confrontation. Something had to give and it wasn't going to be us. At the moment that the RUC smashed their way into the crowd in Duke Street it was as if all the small things that had been happening suddenly came together in a more coherent and a more ominous shape. The civil rights movement, the creation of the republican leadership, was out of their control. There would be no turning back. What had started as a campaign for civil rights was developing into the age-old struggle for national rights.

From Reform to Revolution

An té nach bhfuil láidir ní foláir dhó bheith glic.
(*If you are not strong you had best be cunning.*)

AS PART OF the 'United Kingdom of Great Britain and Northern Ireland' the 6 county state was part of 'British democracy', enjoying some of the fruits of progressive British social legislation, and it was an administrative sub-section of one of the most prominent states in developed, modern, capitalist Europe. Such was the appearance and, to an extent, the reality, yet a profound contradiction existed: this was an apartheid state in which a very substantial minority of the citizens were disenfranchised and denied social, economic, political and civil equality. It was a state fashioned by sectarian power and privilege, a state which practised wholesale suppression and discrimination.

Confronted by the civil rights movement the contradiction exploded in the face of the British government and the state rapidly began to come apart at the seams. A generation of people stood up, cried 'enough' and found the means to build a popular and implacable resistance to inequality and oppression. Previous generations had attempted to develop resistance, had opposed the state and its powers of suppression; republican activists had devoted lifetimes to the struggle and some had lost their lives in the fight. But their struggle had been isolated; carried out by small numbers of dedicated individuals, it had never been based on a broad sector of the population which was determined not only that change should come about but that it could and must come about. Catholics in the 6 counties had been as substantially opposed to the state before but, abandoned under the terms of the Partition Act, few had believed that they could achieve any significant change in the situation.

Some date the watershed to 5 October 1968, others to January 1969; the precise date is unimportant. What was exposed was that in the late twentieth century in the developed, modern European world, an utterly outdated, undemocratic regime was engaged in the violent suppression of those who were seeking the elementary demands of western democracy.

* * *

Whatever outward trappings of statehood the 6 counties have ever possessed they have always been completely subservient to the British government at Westminster. The position is summed up in Article 75 of the Government of Ireland Act (1920):

> Notwithstanding the establishment of the Parliament of Northern Ireland, or anything contained in this Act, the supreme authority of the Parliament of the United Kingdom shall remain unaffected and undiminished over all persons, matters and things in Northern Ireland and every part thereof.

It is a position which is expressed with admirable clarity and which has often been restated.

In recent years the British government has attempted to suggest to international public opinion that Northern Ireland is attached to the United Kingdom by nothing more durable or binding than the will of the majority of its inhabitants. Nothing could be further from the truth: all relevant Acts exclude any right to secession, and the Northern Ireland Constitution Act (1973) states that 'It is hereby declared that Northern Ireland remains part of Her Majesty's Dominions of the United Kingdom'.

The British attitude to the Northern state was prefigured in the approach of leading British politicians prior to its establishment. In July 1912 Bonar Law, leader of the Conservative Party, declared, 'I can imagine no lengths of resistance to which Ulster will go in which I will not be ready to support them'. Lloyd George in May 1916 wrote to Edward Carson, 'We must make sure that Ulster does not, whether she wills it or not, merge with the rest of Ireland.'

In instituting the statelet and in imposing partition, the British goverment also instituted the full apparatus of sectarianism. The armed wing of Protestant Unionism was institutionalised in the form of the 'A', 'B' and 'C' Specials, which were armed, uniformed, organised and paid for by the British government. In the process of consolidating the British state in the 6 counties

475 Irish people were killed and 1,766 injured in two years. In Belfast, 11,000 of the city's Catholics were put out of their jobs and 23,000 were driven from their homes; republicans were executed by RUC murder gangs and internment was widely used.

In the 1960s people of my generation, even those who, like me, came from republican backgrounds, were aware only in the vaguest terms of how the state had been established. When Ian Paisley began his anti-Catholic crusade, when Catholic areas were attacked by the RUC and Peter Ward was killed we heard some of the old people say that this kind of thing had happened before. But we were young and like most young people I suppose we believed that the lessons of the past were of little enough relevance to the immediacy of the present. We understood very little about the workings and dynamics of the state and of Unionism. Nevertheless, it was clear even to us that the 6 counties was a puppet state, subservient to the British government, that nothing went on without the underlying and express approval of the British.

The Stormont parliament was in reality a menial regime and was debarred from legislating in relation to:

The Crown, peace and war, the armed forces, treaties with foreign states, treason, naturalisation, trade with any place outside Northern Ireland, radio, air navigation, lighthouses, coinage, weights and measures, copyrights and patents.

All the appurtenances, in other words, of statehood were denied to the Stormont 'government' and were retained by Westminster. It was also denied control of the Post Office, savings banks and about 90% of its own taxation. What powers it did possess — over justice, policing, land purchase, agriculture and housing — could be withdrawn at any time.

The role of the Stormont government was to maintain the status quo, to carry out on the ground the logic of the partition that had ensured a permanent majority for the Unionists by ceding three of Ulster's nine counties to the Dublin government. One-party rule was established and was guaranteed almost immediately by a system of ward-rigging and voting qualifications; proportional representation was abolished, business votes were established and franchise was limited at local government level to ratepayers and their wives. Unionists were placed in control of the entire political system. As part of the control of votes, Catholics were denied equal access to housing, and as part of the control of population — and thus of votes — Catholics were denied equal access to employment.

When the British government introduced universal suffrage, abolishing the restricted franchise for local government in 1945, the Stormont government secured the exclusion of the 6 counties from the provisions of the legislation. They also went beyond that by introducing in 1946 their own Representation of the People Bill which restricted the franchise even more by taking the vote away from lodgers who were not ratepayers and retained company voting whereby up to six votes were allocated to the directors of limited companies. The thinking behind this legislation was eloquently expressed by Major L.E. Curran, the government Chief Whip: 'The best way to prevent the overthrow of the government by people who had no stake in the country and had not the welfare of the people of Ulster at heart was to disenfranchise them.'

To keep the lid on a blatantly oppressive system coercive legislation was introduced with the full approval, of course, of the British government. Under the Civil Authorities (Special Powers) Act the Civil Authority (the Minister for Home Affairs) and the RUC were empowered to:

1. Arrest without warrant.
2. Imprison without charge or trial and deny recourse to a court of law or to Habeas Corpus.
3. Enter and search homes without warrant and with force, any time of the day or night.
4. Declare a curfew and prohibit meetings, assemblies, fairs, markets and processions.
5. Permit flogging as punishment.
6. Deny claim to trial by jury.
7. Arrest persons it is desired to examine as witness, forcibly detain them and compel them to answer questions, under penalties, even if answers may incriminate them. Such a person is guilty of an offence if he refuses to be sworn or answer a question; this applies even when no offence is known, provided a police officer has reason to believe that one 'is about to be committed'.

8. Do any act involving interference with the rights of private property.

9. Prevent access of relatives or legal advisors to a person imprisoned without trial.

10. Prohibit the holding of an inquest after a prisoner's death.

11. Arrest a person 'who by word of mouth' spreads false reports or makes false statements.

12. Prohibit the circulation of any newspaper.

13. Prohibit the possession of any film or gramophone record.

14. Forbid the erection of any monument or other memorial.

15. Enter the premises of any bank, examine accounts, and order the transfer of money, property, vouchers or documents to the Civil Authority. If the bank fails to comply an offence is committed.

16. Arrest a person who does anything 'calculated to be prejudicial to the preservation of peace or maintenance of order in Northern Ireland and not specifically provided for in the regulations.'

The Civil Authority was the Stormont Minister of Home Affairs and he was empowered to delegate the powers granted him under the Act to any RUC man he wished, and he was also authorised to make new regulations and new laws without consulting parliament. The Special Powers Act, as it became known, was renewed every year from its inception in 1922 until 1928 when it was renewed every five years; it eventually became permanent in 1933 and was superceded in 1973 by the Northern Ireland (Emergency Provisions) Act. Such powers, fully sanctioned by the British government, were no mere passive presence in the background; they were the active means by which the existence of the state was maintained and all opposition was suppressed. Organisations, meetings and newspapers were banned. Curfews were imposed, whole (Catholic) areas were searched, and internment without trial was used in 1920-21, 1922-4, 1938-45, 1956-61, 1969 and 1971-5.

It is hardly surprising to learn that Mr Vorster, who was then South African Minister for Justice, remarked in 1963 that he 'would be willing to exchange all the legislation of that sort [Coercion Acts] for one clause of the Northern Ireland Special Powers Act.'

People such as myself knew little about the precise provisions of the law; we simply absorbed a general awareness that if they wanted to get you they could, that power in all situations rested with them — with the state, the RUC, the law courts. We were not of a class that understood terms such as *habeas corpus* and while we were aware that the Campaign for Social Justice and others were complaining about the state of affairs, we had no real understanding of how the Unionist system worked.

Blatant discrimination in access to jobs and housing allocation was something one took for granted, almost like part of the landscape. In 1969 out of 209 people employed in the technical and professional grades of the civil service only 13 were Catholics; of the 319 employed in the higher administrative grades only 23 were Catholics. Of the 115 people nominated by the government to serve on nine public boards only 16 were Catholics. Yet I registered the fact that the conditions I knew in the Falls were similar to those I saw in the Shankill Road and the Old Lodge Road, both Protestant areas; the conditions in Catholic Ballymurphy were similar to those in Protestant Moyard. The fact was that conditions in the 6 counties for working class people were pitiable, irrespective of whether they were Protestant or Catholic.

As I absorbed all of this I came to understand the centrality of partition in the whole dreadful scheme. I also realised that without a proper understanding of the reason and consequences of partition there could be no understanding of the problem and thus no solution. Partition was, and remains, the main means by which equality is denied us and the principal method by which self-determination is withheld from us. Partition aborted a national independence struggle in the 1920s, secured Britain a toehold in part of Ireland from which she could influence all of Ireland; it divided the Irish people into two states, and within one state it established a Unionist monopoly which divided us once more.

*   *   *

The break-up of monolithic Unionism in the late 1950s began as a result of moves initiated by Unionism in its own self-interest. When the linen and ship-building industries were in their heydays, which coincided largely with the two World Wars, there had been an industrial base in the north-east of Ulster which was integrated into British and British Empire markets. This provided the economic foundation of the narrow concept of Unionist self-interest which was expressed in the notion of Stormont as 'a Protestant parliament for a Protestant people'. The Unionist Party was then the property of the landed gentry, people who probably would have felt more at home in the British House of Lords and who were in many instances related to the British aristocracy.

When Terence O'Neill took over as Prime Minister from Lord Brookeborough in March 1963 the basis for the old narrow self-interest had already been succeeded by a new dynamic. The linen and ship-building industries were in steep decline and O'Neill, a former Minister of Finance, perceived the need to attract multinational capital. The evidently antiquated social relations which characterised the 6 county state did not appeal to the British, European and US companies he sought to attract in the build-up to EEC membership and in the wake of the decline of the British Empire, and so he tried to modernise the style of government and to project an image of the state which was more in tune with the twentieth century.

The process required at least an appearance of some kind of partnership, both in relation to the other state on the island, the 26 counties, and in relation to the minority which had been so systematically excluded from having an equal role in the society of the 6 counties. The most obvious grievances of the nationalist population and the crudest facets of Unionism gave the Dublin government a problem. The Prime Minister of the 26 counties, Sean Lemass, could not afford to be seen to deal with people who were blatantly mistreating a sizeable section of the population. And this led to a new era of Unionism characterised by certain liberal noises which were expressed not just by Terence O'Neill but also by publications such as the *Belfast Telegraph*, which had previously expressed a traditional Protestant ascendancy perspective.

All political ideology is based on either the self-interest of those who support it or on what they *perceive* to be their self-interest. The self-interest of Unionism was to keep the papists down. This playing of the Orange card, this exploitation of the perceived self-interest of working class Unionists, was an essential element in keeping Unionism intact and united; and despite social contradictions between elements of its support is still remained a monolith, firmly set on the foundation of supremacist ideology.

When O'Neill tried to alter the appearance of the state he ran into major difficulties. There were two reasons for this: firstly, those who saw their self-interest as being sectarian, narrow and anti-papist rose up against any such liberalisation, even when its value was explained to them in the most schoolmasterly language. It was at that point that one found Ian Paisley throwing snowballs outside Stormont at Sean Lemass's cavalcade. The second reason for O'Neill's difficulties, which was totally coincidental in relation to this development in Unionism, was the rise of the civil rights movement.

O'Neill has largely escaped criticism and has in a quite unrealistic manner been portrayed as a liberal who, if only he had been given a chance, would have achieved social progress. A rather parochial answer to that view is provided by what a man said to me one day several years ago in the Falls Road. 'I don't mind a bigot,' he said, 'because a bigot doesn't know any better. I don't mind a bigot but I can't stand an educated bigot.' Terence O'Neill was an educated bigot. He was just sophisticated enough to know that the self-interest of Unionism could no longer be sustained by the crude methods of the past, but the Orange monster which Unionism and the British colonial ethos had created could not take the change. At the same time, the demand for ordinary civil rights could not be dealt with, as it had been previously, by straightforward coercion.

An important factor in the difficulties which Unionism faced with the civil rights movement was television. For example, in the early '60s Brian Faulkner had been engaged in aggressive provocations in the Longstone Road, but they were not covered by television. The RUC action on 5 October 1968 was not the first action of its kind by any means, but it was the first time that such brutality had been enacted in front of television cameras. Years later, the killing of John Downes was by no means unique: other people had been killed by plastic bullets; thousands of rounds had been fired; numerous people had been injured. The killing of John Downes was different because it was seen by the media. The fact was that in the electronic age Unionism and later the British could not cover up all that was happening.

O'Neill's attempt to modernise the appearance of the state, combined with the rise of the civil rights movement, began the break-up of the Unionist monolith as the cover-all philosophy which had been able to unite all kinds of different strands and strata. When it had suffered small cracks in the past — when the NILP had been able to win Protestant votes, for example — it had cemented itself again with the glue of sectarianism. It could do this easily when it did not have to make any gestures of goodwill towards its non-citizens, the Catholics. These days were now gone, and the divisions within Unionism widened as a result.

O'Neill attacked the Burntollet march as 'a foolhardy and irresponsible undertaking' and civil rights marchers as 'mere hooligans'. He ignored the violence inflicted upon peaceful demonstrators by the sticks and stones of loyalists, ignored the fact that about a hundred of the ambushers were members of the 'B' Specials, ignored the assault by drunken RUC men on the Bogside in Derry. Instead, he warned that he would mobilise the 'B' Specials. Yet despite O'Neill's vitriol against the civil rights marchers he found himself under attack from the extreme right. In an attempt to bolster his position he called an election for 24 February 1969, hoping to emerge with an increased number of his supporters in Stormont. It was an election which saw the Nationalist Party lose ground to civil rights candidates, but more importantly in terms of Unionism the election exacerbated the tensions within the Unionist Party between pro- and anti-O'Neill factions and heralded the emergence of the fledgling Paisleyite party. The fundamentalist branch of Unionism had begun to achieve new prominence.

The Unionist party had always enjoyed the support of the disparate elements in the Protestant community because it had been able to ward off any threat to Protestant privilege. For centuries the Protestants had been told that they were the chosen people and that the Catholics were scum. 'I wouldn't have one about the place,' said Prime Minister Brookeborough. Religious demagogues pumped out their message of hatred against 'the purple whore' and the 'fenians breeding like rats'. The reactionary nature of Unionism grows from the fact that they have to defend the indefensible. When one cannot defend one's position in an honest and rational way one naturally adopts a kind of laager mentality and forgets about trying to convert world opinion. In this sense the Unionists have the same problem as the white regime in South Africa.

Terence O'Neill (later the great white hope of Dublin middle class opinion as represented by *The Irish Times*) expressed his own difficulties in terms which achieved a typical combination of condescension and prejudice.

> It is frightfully hard to explain to Protestants that if you give Roman Catholics a good job and a good house they will live like Protestants, because they will see their neighbours with cars and television sets.
>
> They will refuse to have eighteen children, but if a Roman Catholic is jobless and lives in the most ghastly hovel, he will rear eighteen children on National Assistance . . .
>
> If you treat Roman Catholics with due consideration and kindness they will live like Protestants, in spite of the authoritative nature of their church.

Little wonder O'Neill failed to convince anyone, not least his fellow Unionists. Not only did they successfully depose him but in classic coup d'état style they blasted electricity installations and the Silent Valley reservoir in the process. The IRA, which was blamed for these operations, during this time had to content itself with petrol bombing a number of Belfast post offices in retaliation for the beating to death of Samuel Devenny by the RUC in Derry.

The Unionists appeared to have everything, even bigger bombs. Nevertheless I, for one, did not have a clear understanding then of what Unionism was and certainly did not identify any of the ordinary Protestants I met daily as having anything to do with the open sectarianism and coercion of the state.

In rural areas it was different. There the folk memory of the perceived superiority of political Protestantism over Catholics remains very strong to this day. People can show you the land that was taken off their family three or four hundred years ago and they will name the families that took it. In fact, this is not unique to the 6 counties; one finds it all over Ireland. The indigenous population were dispossessed of their land by planters and from time to time these planters had to fight tooth and nail to retain that land by means of various forms of coercion, including the Penal Laws. These laws effectively created an apartheid system with the Catholics placed in basically the same situation as the blacks in South Africa today. In terms of the land, the oldest male child of a family could only inherit land if he converted to Protestantism; otherwise the land passed to all the male heirs. This quickly reduced the size and viability of Catholic-owned farms.

In modern times this apartheid system was supported at every turn by the assurances of senior British political figures or the British government itself. The institutionalised form which their assurances took was the loyalist veto. Unionists refused, and refuse still, to deal with their Catholic neighbours as equals because they didn't need to. Unlike their black counterparts in South Africa, however, the Irish Catholic labour force, both rural and urban, wasn't necessary for the well-being of the state. Deserted by Dublin, displaced persons in their own country, they had no political or economic muscle with which to gain equality. And the refusal of the Unionists, though I didn't understand it then, was in the circumstances understandable from their point of view. They had been told by the British government that their privileged position as an ascendancy would remain for as along as the Union with Britain remained and that would be for as long as they desired it. As if to underline this, in April 1969 five hundred extra British troops were flown in from England to guard installations against further IRA attacks. The attacks, of course, had been the work of the UVF.

In the beginning I was puzzled by all this and by the state's reaction to even the most passive form of dissent. Why should we be forbidden to sell our newspaper, to wear an Easter lily, to fly a tricolour flag? Why couldn't jobs be provided and what was so rebellious about asking this? What was so treasonable about demanding a decent home? Where was the subversion in the demand for equal voting rights?

I did not have a very clear understanding of the Northern Ireland state, of what it was. Our housing agitation was as much aimed against the old nationalist politicians and their failure; they seemed to be involved in a very sterile, do-a-favour-for-a-constituent type of politics. We were taking an approach that the people have a right to a house so let's get them a house. Being young and enthusiastic we didn't see why we should have to wait when you could go into the Housing Trust and do a sit-in and get results. It wasn't clear to me in the beginning that the housing problem had anything to do with the state as such or even with voting.

At that time there was cross-community communication, which I don't want to exaggerate, but it was there. I knew a lot of Protestants, I worked in a Protestant area; there were differences, but they seemed only to come to the surface around the Twelfth. But even then I watched Twelfth of July parades and bonfires and I enjoyed them. The nasty side of sectarianism hadn't manifested itself yet.

It was only as I started to meet reactions that I started to ask why: why did small things lead to over-reaction? Over the Sherlock squat a number of us got something like 57 summonses; at that time we laughed about it, but in retrospect it was a gross over-reaction. The RUC activity of landrovers patrolling the Loney area of West Belfast was a similar over-reaction. When I started to go to debates and listen to people who obviously had well-documented proof of discrimination, I began to go through a process of politicisation, and that, combined with my experience of the reaction of the RUC, pushed me to clarify my views of the situation. I began to realise that Catholics were being denied houses because that meant that they could be denied votes. I discovered that gerrymandering in Derry was a conscious practice carried out to maintain one-party control. In a very parochial sense I began to realise that this kind of sectarianism wasn't just a blind hatred of Catholics but was something which was being used tactically for Unionist political advantage.

I was, as I mentioned before, about 18 months in Sinn Féin before I realised what I was in. Then, as I started to examine the situation I began to see that we were not dealing with just a Unionist hatred of 'papists' but that it was actually in the state's interest to stop, for example, the sale of republican papers, to stop the ideas of republicanism being promoted.

When William Craig reacted immediately in banning the Republican Clubs I realised that the Unionist government were opposed to the organisation of political opinion which was radically different from theirs. Through that process I began to get an understanding of the state. The British government claimed ultimate responsibility over the 6 counties area. It was thus responsible for the situation, but it had deluded public opinion at home and abroad into believing that responsibility rested with the Stormont regime. This regime was refusing to introduce the minimum reforms demanded by the civil rights agitation and the British government was unwilling to force such reforms upon its puppet government. The republican leadership's strategy of progressive democratisation could not succeed in the face of such intransigence. But neither could the British continue to disguise their role. Increasingly they were being forced, by the contradictions inherent within their statelet, into taking a more dominant role. Many of us saw this as a useful development with the potential for ridding us of the barrier administration at Stormont and placing the responsibility clearly where it belonged — with the colonial power in London.

In 1963 I hadn't even been sure what the border was. Going to the Donegal Gaeltacht, I looked out to see where the border was and what it looked like. I didn't know in 1960 or 1961 what the IRA was. I remember myself and a friend in school trying to work it out and deciding it was the Irish Rebel Army. There was a certain bravado in singing a rebel song, in shouting something at the RUC. There was the famous case of a fella known as 'Throw-the-Brick'. He was working on a building site and when the British Queen came to Belfast on a visit he threw a brick at her. Everybody wanted to meet him and when he came out of prison you'd be delighted if you saw him on the street because he was famous, but you didn't really understand what it was all about. It was enough to know that it wasn't our Queen he'd thrown the brick at. The only face of Unionist power I really encountered was the RUC; in rural areas harassment by the 'B' Specials was a constant fact of life, but in Belfast they were not a particularly significant feature.

Most working class Catholics were overwhelmingly fatalistic and apathetic. One older man, a veteran of the IRA's 1930s campaign, was unaffected by my youthful zeal and probably spoke for most of his generation when one day he told me wearily: 'Never bother yourself. It'll be all the same in a thousand years.' People weren't politicised, most were finding it hard to make ends meet and there was a high level of emigration. But the feeling of isolation, of alienation from the state, was not confined to the Catholic working class who were mostly resigned to their fate. The professional class were also affected.

A new generation of young Catholics with expectations of being able to rise socially, having fulfilled the educational requirements, found it difficult to accept the status quo which denied them their place in the sun. The student radicals, most prominent of whom was Bernadette Devlin, were articulate and defiant; they weren't going to be chased back into the ghettoes and they were well able to state their case on television. This new element combined with others to act as a catalyst for the mobilisation of the non-Unionist population.

The state at any time could have undermined the civil rights agitation by moving swiftly on what were normal democratic demands; and perhaps in the global sense if wider issues had occurred earlier the natural consequence of EEC membership would have been to modernise the state. But movement came too late. In fact, whatever civil rights reforms were granted were only granted after the holocaust, after the whole thing was up in the air.

By 1969, well before the pogroms, I sensed that we were playing with something extraordinarily dangerous. I had numerous arguments with Liam McMillen because I didn't think that the Belfast or Dublin leaderships understood what was happening. They appeared unable to give proper direction in the face of the small riot situations which were beginning to develop in Ardoyne and Unity Flats. Elsewhere throughout the 6 counties tensions were also rising. The RUC, the 'B' Specials and loyalist counter-demonstrators were clashing frequently with Catholic civilians. In July renewed attacks by the RUC in the Bogside area of Derry lasted three days and in Dungiven they batoned a Catholic man to death.

Our agitation around Divis Flats was becoming a series of ever more frequent skirmishes with the RUC, whose ferocity was a revelation. The particularly frightening aspect of it was that we, the small group of republican activists, had been identified by this stage as leading the local agitations so that — and I've had this experience many times since — we found ourselves as we ran like hell looking over our shoulders at the baton chargers passing other protestors and obviously heading for the republicans, heading for us.

I felt, in the eye of the storm, that we were moving rapidly towards catastrophe and I was absolutely frustrated that the people who were in the leadership of the republican movement did not appear to understand what was happening. Maybe they did. Maybe I was too young and too dogmatic.

I remember on one occasion at Hastings Street barracks, where there was frequent rioting, there was a baton charge and people turned to face it and the RUC fled back into the barracks. We then proceeded to the barracks door and, armed with a telegraph pole, about fifty of us started to use the pole as a battering ram against the door and then, through a series of shouts, another fella and myself were accepted in as a delegation. There was a feeling of recklessness, that we had them, and we relished that feeling. I saw the same thing later, in 1971 in Ballymurphy, where young people went into the barracks there and drove out the British Army landrovers.

Being nineteen or twenty years old and not having any responsibilities; being fit enough to go and spend three, four or five nights in succession, sitting in a squat, going to Unity Flats, to Hooker Street and in between times off for a weekend in Dublin or to a fleadh: there was a sense of freedom, a youthful, naive and mistaken feeling that the revolution was happening all around us and that the world was beginning to respond. By July we were actively involved in trying to get people in Ardoyne and Unity Flats organised to defend themselves against further RUC and loyalist attacks during the Orange parades. In the meantime the republican leadership was in no way prepared for any sort of military defence, never mind an offensive. It was instead engaged in semantics.

By August the balloon was up. There were days of heavy rioting in Ardoyne and in Unity Flats. Patrick Corry, a Catholic, was beaten to death in an RUC barracks. The first Catholic families were being intimidated out of the Crumlin Road area by loyalist gangs. In Derry a Bogside Defence Association had been established by republicans in preparation for expected loyalist and RUC attacks during the annual loyalist parade on 12 August.

On 8 August Prime Minister Chichester Clarke, his Home Affairs Minister and James Callaghan the British Prime Minister met in London to discuss the situation. British troops were put on stand-by in Derry and Belfast in support of the Unionist regime. The highly provocative loyalist march was going ahead and the 'croppies' were expected to lie down once again. But they didn't. Instead, the battle of the Bogside began.

RUC armoured cars attacked the Bogside barricades and for the first time CS gas was used. Defenders hurled stones, bricks, broken paving slabs and petrol bombs and the tricolour flew from a tower block alongside the flag of James Connolly's Irish Citizen Army, the Starry Plough. The siege continued day and night, but even with a force of 700 at their command, with armoured cars, batons and CS gas the RUC could not subdue the Bogside.

On the second day at an emotional meeting of NICRA in Belfast we heard a tape-recorded plea from the Bogside for help. A proposal to draw the RUC out of Derry or at least to prevent reinforcements being sent in was enthusiastically endorsed. Rallies were to be organised throughout the 6 counties. On behalf of the West Belfast Housing Action Committee I informed the meeting that we would hold a protest march and meeting on the Falls Road. A NICRA delegation was later to go to Stormont to plead for the withdrawal of the RUC from the Bogside. We left the meeting to make petrol bombs. The NICRA request was refused and the 6 counties erupted.

At 5pm on 14 August British troops entered Derry and took up positions. The RUC and 'B' Specials were pulled back and the troops remained outside the Bogside. In Belfast barricades had been erected on the Falls Road. Loyalist mobs, in many instances led by 'B' Specials, attacked and burned Catholic houses. The RUC, with Shorland armoured cars and Browning heavy machine guns, fired into Divis Flats; in Ardoyne they opened up with sub-machine guns. Seven people were killed in loyalist and RUC attacks, including John Gallagher who was shot dead in Armagh by the 'B' Specials. The IRA had virtually no guns with which to resist the attacks, but a small number of weapons was mustered and played a role in driving the loyalists and Specials out of the Falls Road.

Arms were rushed up from the 26 counties and barricades were strengthened to meet the continuing loyalist attacks. British troops took up positions on the Falls Road; they did not intervene to take down barricades but neither did they intervene when loyalists burned down the whole of Catholic Bombay Street and a young Fianna boy, Gerard McCauley, was killed trying to defend the street. As the RUC and loyalists attacked Ardoyne another Catholic street, Brookfield Street, was burned down. In all, 1,820 families left their homes in Belfast, 1,505 of them Catholics, during July, August and September.

* * *

The situation had developed rapidly. The demands of the civil rights movement had been demands for rights which were taken for granted in western Europe and they were demands for rights which existed in the the rest of the so-called United Kingdom. In retrospect they were, in themselves, unremarkable, simple and moderate demands. Yet they had evoked a ferocious response from the state and its supporters and the consequence of that response had left the authority and stability of the state in tatters. When I had first become involved in political action I had asked myself what was so rebellious about asking for jobs; what was so treasonable about demanding a decent home; what was so subversive about seeking equal voting rights. I had received my answer, as had we all.

The civil rights movement had been looking for democratisation of the state, but the state had made abundantly clear the fact that it would not and could not implement democratic reforms. The movement had placed its demands on the state; it had not demanded the abolition of the state, nor a United Ireland. Now, however, with the reaction of the state and the intervention of the British army, the constitutional question had come to the fore and the whole existence of the 6 county state stood in question.

The republican strategy of organising politically to achieve democracy within the state, which had involved a turning away from the physical force tradition and a dumping of arms, had run headlong into the reality of the irreformably sectarian state. That the republican movement now turned to armed resistance had nothing to do with any ingrained militarism but had everything to do with the stark realities of the situation.

The republican movement of the 1960s had proved incapable of responding adequately to events as they evolved in the 6 counties. The spontaneous popular uprising of August 1969 — uncoordinated, locally organised, lacking any general plan — and the subsequent effects in the 26 counties found the movement ill-prepared and unable to cope with the needs and potential of that period.

Failure and inadequacy did not relate solely to the question of defence for beleagured nationalist areas. Indeed, lack of guns was not a primary problem as it was made up quite rapidly. The primary problem was lack of politics, a shortcoming which was to remain even after guns had become plentiful.

This lack of politics, affecting all tendencies in the then disunited republican movement, arose from an inability to understand what was happening on the ground, its causes, effects and possible consequences. Many of those who warned, quite correctly, of the need for armed defence contingencies, many of those who were strident in their condemnation of the republican leadership's failure to provide such necessities did not understand the political requirements of that time. But the leadership was clearly lacking in political understanding and this led to their failure to prepare properly on all fronts, not least on the question of defence.

Understandably in the circumstances, their failure was seen simply in terms of military preparedness, and this view, allied to a suspicion amongst the older republicans of the politicisation process in which the movement was engaged, led to the split in 1970, a major set-back for the republican cause. It also ensured that the reinvigorated republican struggle which emerged then was an inadequate one because the only republican organisation which arose from the ashes was a military one: it had little or no proper educational process, no formal politicisation courses and there was scant regard paid by the leadership to such needs.

Everyone connected with the movement at that time was, of course, responsible for such shortcomings, and perhaps the situation could not have been otherwise. As in the case of any radical movement, republicans have had to grapple not only with the movement's historical shortcomings but with the whole question of finding a strategy for moving towards the independent republic. This is an on-going task requiring continuous analysis, co-education, good internal and external communications, reassessments, flexibility and, most of all, agreement on the final objective. At some stage in the late '60s the republican leadership lost sight of most, if not all, of these requirements, and the lessons of that period are as important today as ever. Any leadership which ignores these lessons will, like the Goulding leadership, do so at a terrible cost to itself and the people it seeks to serve.

Politics in the 26 Counties

> A political revolution in Ireland without a coinciden-
> tal economic revolution simply means a change of
> masters. . . If the Irish people do not control Irish in-
> dustries, transport, money and the soil of the coun-
> try, then foreign and native capitalists will. And
> whoever controls the wealth of a country and the pro-
> cess by which wealth is attained will also control its
> government.
>
> *Liam Mellows*

THE NORTHERN NATIONALIST looking at the 26 counties is not impressed. From the perspective of an Irish person in a British state — a dispossessed and a disadvantaged person — the 26 county state looks pretty sick, its political life even more so. Poverty stares at you, with conditions in some working class areas no better than the conditions in the 6 counties about which the Dublin government today express so much concern. In a town in County Longford I have seen a street that looked as if it belonged in the last century. Dublin's inner city poverty backs onto the contrasting world of the large stores, hotels and burger joints of O'Connell Street where beggars abound. Travellers are harassed by reactionary mobs and by the gardai in almost every part of the state. At least in the 6 counties the nationalist people have a certain advantage in that they can if they wish become involved in the struggle which seeks to end their conditions of poverty and discrimination; they can at least, while suffering all the indignities of their position, experience the dignity of struggle. But this opportunity is, so far, at any rate, basically lacking in the 26 counties.

The sad truth of James Connolly's perception is evident in every sphere of public life in the 26 counties. In 1897 Connolly warned:

If you remove the English Army tomorrow and hoist the green flag over Dublin Castle, unless you set about the organisation of a Socialist Republic your efforts would have been in vain. England would still rule. She would rule you through the whole array of commercial and individualist institutions she has planted in this country and watered with the tears of our mothers and the blood of our martyrs.

England would still rule you, even while your lips offered hypocritical homage at the shrine of that freedom whose cause you have betrayed.

I naturally meet many old republicans and it is quite clear that not only do they see the 6 counties as representing unfinished business but that the 26 counties is not even a shadow of the republic they worked and fought for. One startling symbol is the naming of the appalling tower blocks of Ballymun after Pearse and MacDonagh. And if one wishes to assess the reality of the 26 counties against the politics of those who were engaged in the national revolution, one cannot but register the disparity between, for example, Pearse's educational ideas and the education system as it has been developed.

One must judge everyone in the context of their times and Pearse's St Enda's school project and his educational ideas are still radical today; what, one wonders, must they have been like in his own time? His book, *The Murder Machine*, was a magnificent exposé of the educational system and, if one employs it as a barometer of what changes have taken place one must conclude that the murder machine is still with us seventy years later. There has always been a blatant hypocrisy in the 26 county state holding up Patrick Pearse as a national hero while clearly contradicting all the tenets of his philosophy. But now there is a more dangerous development in the fact that since revisionism has become thoroughly established in the schools the next generation may not even know who Patrick Pearse was, let alone what his ideas were.

Leinster House is the preserve, by and large, of unprincipled careerists jockeying for the Ministerial Mercedes, using the taxpayers' money to send Christmas cards to constituents, pretending to have obtained for constituents housing that should be theirs by right and which they actually obtained through no effort of any TD, voting themselves automatic salary increases, earning large pensions long before any thoughts of retirement. . . The list is endless and quite rightly inspires no respect amongst the young in particular. At the end of the day what nationalists in the 6 counties know about the main political parties in the Free State is that they are quite prepared to side with the British government rather than seek in any meaningful way to achieve redress of our very substantial grievances as people discriminated against and brutalised by the British administration.

In retrospect one could not expect otherwise than that the 26 county state would develop in a way that was a negation of the national revolution. As Maire Comerford pointed out in *The First Dáil*, all those who had shaped the political philosophy that led to the 1916 Rising were removed in the executions after the Rising. And following their removal the counter-revolutionaries took over.

The leadership of the republican struggle passed effectively into the control of non-republicans — Arthur Griffith, Michael Collins, Eamon de Valera and others who merely wished for a change in the economic management of the country. They, and the business interests they represented, wished to become the new management and they came into power on the backs of a national revolution — on other men's wounds, as Ernie O'Malley so succinctly put it.

What was established in 1920-22 was a new scheme to control Ireland, a partitionist scheme which was to have its effects in the 26 counties as surely as in the 6 counties. In the 6 counties we have a colonial situation. In the 26 counties we have a neo-colonial state in which the imperial foreign government was exchanged for a native one based on business interests which were satisfied to work the old system provided that it was modified sufficiently to ensure its continued existence.

The 1921 arrangement gave the Free State limited political power within a dominion status. The new state had all the symbols of freedom but little of the real substance of freedom; although some advances were made in subsequent years by successive Dublin governments no advance has been made on the national question and so it remains today. There was and remains no change in the civil service, the judicial system or in legislation. There was merely a change of managers. As Lord

Birkenhead described it, the treaty arrangement was 'protecting British interests with an economy of British lives'.

The declaration of social intent in the 1916 Proclamation and the revolutionary programme of the First Dáil were abandoned. To be sure, there had been little serious effort to implement them, but now they were set aside completely. Partition was a division of territory and of people and a denial of national sovereignty and self-determination. Yet the economic control remained unpartitioned: it remained securely in the hands of its previous owners and there was a free movement of capital. England still ruled us 'through the whole array of commercial and individualist institutions she had planted in this country'.

The Cumann na nGael government which ruled the new Free State from 1922 to 1932 represented the most pro-imperialist elements in the state. Their economic interests in commerce, banking, trade, large farming concerns, brewing and distilling, or in sections of the higher professional groups, required free trade with Britain and close political and cultural ties with her. It was not that they sold out the republic of 1916: as Liam Mellows said of them at that time, 'the men with a stake in the country were never for the republic'. Mellows, like Connolly, possessed great clarity of political vision, and he spelt out what was happening:

Free State equals capitalism and industrialism equals the Empire . . . A political revolution in Ireland without a coincident economic revolution merely means a change of masters. Instead of British capitalism waxing rich on the political and economic enslavement of Ireland we would have Irish capitalists waxing rich on the political freedom but contrived enslavement of Ireland.

And so it came to be. The new Free State government imposed the treaty arrangement with a terrible ferocity greater even than the actions of the new Stormont government in the 6 counties. The new state was moulded in the image of those in control. Not only were nationalists in the 6 counties abandoned but workers and small farmers in the 26 counties gained nothing from the new political arrangement. The Fianna Fáil party which emerged following the counter-revolution of the civil war represented the small manufacturers and distributors as opposed to the bankers, big ranchers and merchants who supported Cumann na nGael (now Fine Gael). These elements, coupled with small farmers and workers who were being starved out by Cumann na nGael's policies and denied a proper political alternative by a largely apolitical IRA, swept Fianna Fáil into power on a broadly anti-imperialist programme which was implemented to a degree in the 1930s.

The economic interests which the Fianna Fáil leadership represented were not content with the treaty arrangement. They wanted not free trade with Britain but a protected home market which they could exploit. They wanted home manufacture rather than imported goods from Britain. They wanted a protected Irish industry and a restriction of the freedom that British industry had enjoyed in Ireland since the Union. By and large Griffiths' old protectionist policies suited their needs.

Yet Fianna Fáil, the party of the industrial middle class and always prone to compromise with British imperialism, received support from the workers and small farmers. They, for their part, had little alternative: Labour was 'waiting'; the IRA was suspicious of 'politics'. Fianna Fáil filled the gap with republican rhetoric. But for all its rhetoric and some advances away from dominion status the Fianna Fáil leadership refused to tackle the partition issue in a meaningful way which could have led to independence.

Nevertheless, the rhetoric of de Valera was a potent force. Put crudely, his public attitude was that Fianna Fáil would achieve Irish reunification; the IRA were going about it the wrong way and had to be moved to one side because they constituted an obstacle. However rhetorical it may have been, it was a difficult argument for republicans to deal with when it was articulated by a national leader of Dev's undoubted stature and when they had failed to establish political alternatives to Fianna Fáil-ism.

When I first became interested in politics and read about de Valera I was mindful of the fact that Fianna Fáil had executed republicans and that Dev, in his application of the coercion acts, had been completely ruthless. Yet I was always intrigued by the meetings he had, even when he was in power, with the Army Council of the IRA. However, its history apart, Fianna Fáil hardly entered my consciousness or that of my contemporaries in

West Belfast until Jack Lynch came out with his famous statement about not standing idly by. When contacts were being made between Fianna Fáil members and 6 county republicans in the aftermath of the 1969 pogroms these were seen as having to do with the Dublin government rather than with Fianna Fáil specifically. (It is worth noting that these contacts were made before the republican split; the contacts were with the Goulding leadership and were maintained by them at least until the movement divided.)

Fianna Fáil moved rapidly under Jack Lynch from the rhetorical assertion of supporting northern nationalists to the closing of Sinn Féin's offices in Dublin and the arrests of prominent Sinn Féin members such as Daithi O'Connell and Ruairi O'Bradaigh. By 1972 most of the nationalistically minded members of the Free State armed forces had been moved either into early retirement or by promotion sideways.

The Fianna Fáil leadership found itself in collision with elements of its own past; it could not continue with republican rhetoric in the face of an actual struggle to bring down the 6 county state. In a more quiescent time it could play the 'green' card to distract attention from difficult social and economic issues, but in the face of an active movement against partition it knew where its true interests lay.

The Fianna Fáil leadership of today has nevertheless remained in touch to some, rhetorical extent with nationalism. One sees, for example, a spontaneous nationalist response at Fianna Fáil Árd Fheiseanna. But even if Charles Haughey is a genuine nationalist who wants to bring about a British withdrawal, Fianna Fáil as it exists now would not have the will to do so. In opposition it has always engaged in nationalist rhetoric, while in government it has in significant periods been cruelly anti-republican and supportive of the British claim to the 6 counties. It may be that the increased sophistication of voters and their general cynicism in relation to the establishment parties will limit Fianna Fáil's ability to exploit the republican instincts of a large section of the population in the way in which they have in the past. What is most interesting about the party today is that it is changing and has changed. More and more in recent years politics in the 26 counties has come to be seen in terms of a good career with numerous perks. People latch themselves onto whatever party seems to offer the best career opportunities, and the result is a breed of TDs which is very different from those that emerged after the Civil War. And the leadership problems of Charles Haughey have been more a product of careerism and small interest groups than anything particularly ideological.

Historically Fine Gael's descent from Cumann na nGael and the fascist Blueshirts makes it a party of political paranoids, ashamed to a degree of its own past. While Fianna Fáil is a law-and-order party with a strong inclination to introduce successive pieces of repressive legislation, Fine Gael has tended to encourage the most blatant use of the gardai to suppress republican opposition. Fine Gael's approach has been to unleash the dogs of war in the form of the political police, giving them more or less carte blanche, as in the case of the 'Heavy Gang', to intimidate and suppress. And they have promoted, with the enthusiastic participation of Conor Cruise O'Brien, the ethos of political censorship.

Garret FitzGerald, leader of Fine Gael, has a pedigree which places him in an awkward position when it comes to condemning the 'men of violence', as both his parents were active in the armed struggle in their time. However, he seems quite unconscious of this awkwardness and ironically casts aspersions instead on the 'flawed pedigree' of Charles Haughey.

FitzGerald is projected as being some kind of liberal, but I cannot for the life of me see what basis exists to view him as being any kind of serious liberal. He was a member of the cabinet during the period of the 'Heavy Gang' and not a squeak of objection was heard from him, and his record in relation to social legislation does not establish any serious claim to liberalism on his part. He launched a 'constitutional crusade' on the radio and that was the last we heard about it. He allowed himself to be pressurised by a backwoods minority pressure group into a constitutional referendum on abortion. He talked about divorce, delayed and postponed action, went and asked the bishops what they thought when everyone already knew what they thought, and then when he did undertake the referendum on divorce he could not even mobilise his own party behind it. If he had tried to implement progressive legislation in a serious manner, as befits a party leader and a prime minister, then one could have a certain respect for him, but he has not. The timing and presentation of his divorce referendum were a mess and his proposition that the 26 counties should be modernised in order to make it more acceptable to the Protestants of the 6 counties is a nonsense. The people now living in the 26 counties deserve to have the legislation that every so often FitzGerald seems to be championing for the benefit of those who are not citizens of the state.

Confronted by the spectacle of the 26 county Labour Party I am almost at a loss for words. I would tend to be very critical of the British Labour Party leadership, especially as regards its bipartisanship with the Tories in relation to Ireland, and I am certainly not an admirer of Neil Kinnock, but one just cannot imagine Kinnock being engaged in a coalition with Margaret Thatcher and presiding over the demolition of the welfare state. Yet this is the direct analogy with what Dick Spring and the Labour Party have been engaged in in the 26 counties. How they can call themselves socialists escapes me. It has been said that the Irish Labour Party went into the GPO in 1916 with James Connolly; unfortunately for the Irish working class, it never came out again.

The leadership of the Labour Party have betrayed the teachings of Connolly, the man who founded the party in 1912. Labour is anti-national and Connolly's proposition that socialists should be to the fore in the national struggle is lost upon the current leadership as surely as it was lost upon their predecessors. After Connolly's death the Labour and trade union leaders opted out of the republican struggle, leaving the political leadership to pass by default to de Valera and Griffith. Since its first coalition with Fine Gael and Clann na Poblachta in 1948 the Labour Party have been instrumental in the revival of Fine Gael and have drifted further to the right in that period. Today's Labour leaders do not even know what the socialist republicanism of Connolly means.

What little radicalism and liberalism exist in Labour circles are by and large long-distance phenomena. An individual such as Michael D. Higgins takes commendable positions in relation to El Salvador, Nicaragua and South Africa, yet he refuses absolutely to face the reality of the struggle going on less than 200 miles from his own doorstep; and he participates in a coalition whose policies cannot be seen as anything other than anti-working class.

Of course, in almost any political system, however corrupt, you will find individuals of integrity and ability. There is no doubt that Michael D. Higgins has qualities which place him apart from the general run of place-seeking careerists. Noel Browne is such an outstanding individual; he is a rare example of a politician showing unimpeachable integrity. But he, again, has to be seen as an individual and, indeed, an individualist whose undoubted qualities do nothing to mitigate the appalling betrayal represented by the Labour Party.

It is symptomatic of the character of the Labour Party that its former leader, Michael O'Leary, should have left it to join the most reactionary party in the state, Fine Gael. Neil Kinnock may have perpetrated a disastrous betrayal of the miners in Britain, but not even his most virulent critic could believe that he would join the Tories. This is what O'Leary did.

The Progressive Democrats, far from 'breaking the mould' of Irish politics as they claim, appear to be offering old wine in old bottles — a fine, right-wing vintage at that. Des O'Malley has been assiduously projected by a significant section of the media as some kind of very liberal figure, yet he is a man who played a key role as Minister for Justice in increasing the Dublin government's array of repressive powers which actually curtail civil liberties, and he has shown no sign whatsoever of making any kind of self-criticism or distancing himself from his record. On the strength of one speech in Leinster House he was hailed as a 'New Republican' (whatever that is). The fact that his very unremarkable speech was so celebrated showed, amongst a number of imponderables, the absolute poverty of political ideas in Leinster House.

What the response to the emergence of the Progressive Democrats shows is the demand for some kind of alternative; the PDs have nothing about themselves to suggest that they will break any kind of mould, but the response does show a very eager wish for an alternative to the established parties. The large attendances at the PDs' meetings were undoubtedly significant; it is probably the first time since the civil war that a new brand of conservatism has emerged. Its origins lie in the patterns of recent change in the 26 counties, in the emergence of an aspiring middle class layer which wants a certain modernisation of some of the social legislation without tampering with the status quo, allied to a large dose of old-fashioned nineteenth century individualistic free enterprise. As regards its position on the national question, O'Malley's anti-republicanism is a matter of public record.

*   *   *

There are many contradictions in the 26 counties which stem basically from the unresolved status of the national question and perhaps the most obvious of these is the survival of instinctive republicanism amongst supporters of every party, despite the policies pursued for years by the leaderships of those parties. I meet members of every party in the 26 counties who are in some sense supporters of the IRA, or who have a sneaking regard for the IRA. At the same time I am well aware of the kind of sentiment which was expressed in the Fine Gael Árd Fheis applause for the capture of the *Marita Anne*. Nevertheless, there is a considerable degree of ambivalence and there is still the emotion of the rebel songs, despite the fact that these are no longer played on RTE. Despite censorship and the massive propaganda effort to disinform and to starve of information, an instinctive republicanism remains.

I find an immense curiosity about the 6 counties amongst young people in the 26 counties. In the course of public meetings, canvassing, debates, seminars and social occasions I find that any articulate republican spokesperson is received without the kind of heckling characteristic of so many meetings, especially those in colleges and universities. It is a strange effect of censorship that, having been projected as having two heads and cloven feet, people find a significance even in the fact of the physical presence of a prominent republican at a meeting. We find that whatever we have to say is listened to with a great amount of interest and whatever questions we are asked are, by and large, genuine questions which seek to explore what it is we stand for.

From meetings with old republicans in the 26 counties I have come away with vivid impressions and with political lessons. When I was invited to address the Kilmichael commemoration a few years ago the response to my acceptance of the invitation was interesting in itself. The event was not organised by members of the republican movement but I met there the last survivors of those who had taken part in the famous ambush. I found that they had been put under great pressure not to attend on account of my presence. The Dublin government had objected, as had the local Catholic bishop, following in the footsteps of his predecessor who had condemned the ambush at the time; also, the customary firing party from the FCA was withdrawn on account of the fact that I would be speaking.

After the speeches I spent the evening with the veterans and I was struck particularly by a remark of a man in his eighties who, in words which had a ring of Liam Mellows about them, said, 'We fought the British to a standstill, and then we proceeded to hand over the politics to others, and they betrayed us.' I was also struck by a strange sense of time warp. Here were people who had been involved in the armed struggle in the Tan War, and they were telling stories about ambushes and incidents which made me feel as if the 6 counties existed in some kind of time capsule along with their own experiences.

These were stories with which I could identify absolutely. Even when they were talking about identity checks, house searches, harassment by the British forces, their stories were almost identical to the stories told amongst republicans in the 6 counties today. One old man cast an interesting light on the way in which the Tan War has been projected as a glorious period in which the Irish people were united behind the IRA against the British army. He spoke about an ambush after which they could find no place to stay: no one would let them in anywhere. In reality it was a small number of republicans who advanced the struggle and it was only when that struggle was about to be successful that it enjoyed mass support.

But what that one evening in West Cork re-impressed upon me most was the great need for the republican movement to develop politically in the 26 counties, the very need that the old man had pointed to in his remark about having left the politics to others. Lack of involvement by republicans in the politics of the 26 counties in the past created a vacuum which was filled by Fianna Fáil. The traditional base of support for republicanism remains in the urban working class and amongst the small farmers, but Fianna Fáil still succeeds in gaining the electoral support of that broadly republican layer.

As a leading member of the Fianna Fáil front bench recently observed to Martin McGuinness, the relationship between Sinn Féin and Fianna Fáil is that of 'second cousins'. Appropriately enough, this remark was made when both men were canvassing in a Dublin by-election. It is a remark which illustrates as well as any lengthy thesis how Fianna Fáil gets its electoral support and how to this day it retains a dominance over the political life of nationalist Ireland. It appeals to the national sentiment and republican instincts.

Fianna Fáil introduced schemes of social welfare, health care and public housing, and in so doing drew support from its working class and small farmer base. Different parts of its programme appeal to different sections of the working people, yet it remains the principal party of native Irish capitalism. The other chief reason for the dominance of Fianna Fáil lies simply in the nature of Irish politics, in its choice of tweedledum or tweedledee in the 26 counties, a distortion caused by the retarding effects of partition and the failure of republicans to provide a relevant alternative in a real republican party with an anti-imperialist programme committed on the national question and to the left of Fianna Fáil.

Charles Haughey speaks now of the need to renegotiate Ireland's relationship with the EEC, he is loud in his condemnation of Sellafield and in expounding on the need for Irish neutrality. Maybe he is serious on these issues. Maybe not. But one can be sure that he is articulating the feelings of sizeable sections of Fianna Fáil supporters who dislike the subservience of their state to the British and other major western governments.

The 26 counties is in a depressing state. Unemployment figures rise daily, with more than 238,000 people now out of work. Thousands are forced to leave. The rate of emigration stands at least at 30,000 a year and probably at more like 50,000 a year; it is as bad now as it was in the 1950s. In the 1930s and 1950s the Dublin government subsidised native capitalists and Irish consumers had to pay higher prices as a result. In the 1950s under the Lemass administration these subsidies were switched from native capitalists to foreign ones, again at the expense of Irish taxpayers. Hundreds of millions of pounds of profits are being exported every year, alongside the export of Irish people.

Since the state was established our natural and mineral

resources have been used to subsidise capitalists, both foreign and domestic. At no time has there been a serious effort to use these resources for the gainful employment and benefit of the mass of Irish people. Irish interests are subordinated to the interests of transnational capital. It could hardly be any other way in a state which was established for 'the protection of British interests with an economy of British lives'. How could it be otherwise when the Dublin government pays about £100 million a year for the maintenance, in contempt of its own constitution, of a British border which all the parties in the 26 counties are pledged to remove? How could it be otherwise when Irish taxpayers pay more for the partition of Ireland than do their counterparts in Britain itself?

The IRA/
Óglaigh na hÉireann

Irishmen and Irishwomen: In the name of God and of the dead generations from which she receives her old tradition of nationhood Ireland, through us, summons her children to the flag and strikes for her freedom.

1916 Proclamation

THE CLASSIC PERIOD of republican struggle, the period which is impressed upon one's mind as the definitive image of the IRA, is the Tan War, with its flying columns taking on the Black and Tans. At its height it was a military campaign with a background of incipient forms of alternative government apparatus functioning through the republican courts in certain parts of the country. The flying columns moved about as fairly self-contained units; they were fed and accommodated in sympathetic households or sometimes they commandeered Unionist houses and lived off the occupants.

In the 1930s and 1940s the IRA enjoyed no such background in the country, and their military actions took place in England, in the 26 counties and only in one or two places in the 6 counties. The 1950s campaign was restricted to the border counties — there was literally no activity in Belfast — and a lot of the IRA people involved came from the 26 counties and presumably worked around the border counties or maintained small flying columns based in Fermanagh, Tyrone and South Armagh. By the end this campaign like those before it consisted of just five or six active republicans skipping between five or six houses.

The current phase of armed struggle is different from any other, apart perhaps from a resemblance to the situation in the Black and Tan War in those areas that enjoyed some kind of governmental status. In the 1970s the struggle developed into a broad political and armed campaign, but even the military aspect developed its own politics of physical force.

What particularly characterises this phase is that the IRA/Óglaigh na hÉireann fights within the occupied area and exists cheek by jowl with the British forces, which have at their command a massive array of technological resources. The IRA today is one of the few guerilla forces in the world which operates in and from within the occupied area, and despite the long duration of this phase of struggle, the IRA continues to enjoy unsurpassed community support.

I wish that physical force had never been part of the political struggle in my lifetime in Ireland. But a statelet which was born in violence has maintained itself throughout its more than sixty years of existence by violence and has been supported in so doing by the British army and government. The conflict which has resulted in the deaths of over 2,500 people began in 1966 with the UVF campaign of assassinations of Catholics; it continued in its early stages with attacks by loyalists and RUC on civil rights marchers and graduated to the joint loyalist/RUC attacks on Catholic streets in Derry and Belfast, and the first member of the RUC to be killed at this time was shot by loyalists on the Shankill Road.

The IRA's armed struggle in this period originated as a defensive response to the combined attacks of the RUC, loyalists and the British army, and it has always been massively outgunned. There are in the 6 counties today something like 123,000 legally held guns, and these are not in the possession of the IRA. There are approximately 30,000 members of the British forces, between British soldiers, the UDR, the RUC and the RUC Reserve. They are armed with sophisticated weapons, with armoured cars, a massive battery of electronic surveillance equipment, with cameras trained on many streets of West Belfast and Derry, and they are backed by the law which, in Brigadier Frank Kitson's phrase, is 'just another weapon in the government's arsenal . . . little more than a propaganda cover for the disposal of unwanted members of the public.'

From defensive origins the IRA campaign developed into an offensive against the state, and there is no denying the fact that innocent bystanders were killed and injured as a consequence of IRA actions. Death by violence is always a sickening tragedy and no talk of 'the inevitable casualties of guerrilla warfare' can do anything to alter the fact. I deeply regret all the deaths and injuries which occur in the course of this struggle and although I have never tried to justify civilian casualties or fatalities of IRA actions I am challenged constantly by some journalists and television interviewers, imitating the attitudes of their political masters, with having placed myself and the whole republican movement outside the bounds of political debate by refusing to condemn the IRA and the IRA is commented upon in an unreal way as if its motivation were the pursuit of violence for its own sake. It is commented upon in a way which ignores and diverts attention away from the circumstances which account both for its origins and for the continuation of its armed activity.

Óglaigh na hÉireann today takes its historical and organisational origins from the forces which engaged in the Easter Rising of 1916, though one can trace its ancestry much further back if one wishes. But the circumstances which shaped the support for the IRA of today are above all the experience of the barricade days from 1969-72. These days are of continuing importance not just in terms of the IRA but because they saw the development of tremendous community solidarity, more than a memory of which remains today.

In response to joint RUC and loyalist attacks nationalist Derry was barricaded from August 1969 until July 1972; in Belfast for a much shorter period there were barricades in up to 26 Catholic enclaves, with the major concentration in West Belfast. Massive shifts in population caused by the loyalist pogroms.— the biggest forced movement of population in Europe since the Second World War — led people to open up their homes behind the barricades to refugees. Everyone had to develop self-reliance and mutual solidarity in order to cope with the situation. Working people took control of aspects of their own lives, organised their own districts, in a way which deeply antagonised and traumatised the Catholic middle class and particularly the Catholic church hierarchy. It was an experience of community oneness, of unselfishness at every hand. And, when more than barricades were required for defence from the armed forces of the RUC, loyalists and, soon, the British army, this generation of the IRA emerged.

The IRA was, in August 1969, disorganised, almost completely unarmed, and unable to play the role it had played in previous pogroms in the 1920s and 30s of defending the areas under attack. In one or two instances firearms were produced by individual republicans in attempts to hold off attacks, but the IRA was in no shape to offer any organised response. Yet by March 1972 the IRA had not only created a defensive force of unprecedented effectiveness, they had also carried out a massive offensive which had succeeded in its aim of bringing down the Stormont government.

In the days, weeks and months after the August 1969 pogroms republicans worked with frantic energy to raise money, to procure arms and to reorganise the IRA to meet the demands of a situation of armed siege. In a remarkably short time a people's army took shape; closely knit with the nationalist community, it was made up of the sons and daughters of ordinary people, its members indistinguishable to any outside observer from the rest of the community. Whether people in the nationalist areas agreed or disagreed with the IRA and all its actions they recognised it as their army, knew for the most part which of their neighbours were members, and referred to it simply as the 'ra'.

Streets, houses, people and even churches were under attack and IRA volunteers — most of whom were very young — put their lives on the line to protect them. At first sticks and stones, petrol bombs and unsophisticated guns were used against the forces of the state, which were equipped with the most up-to-date weaponry. And in the midst of days of rioting and skirmishes the IRA was screening, training and attempting to instil discipline in large numbers of new recruits. Much had to be done under intense pressure and at breakneck speed but before long the IRA had adopted clear structures for its operations and had acquired explosives and guns that stood a chance of generating an effective counter to the firepower being directed against the nationalist areas.

When the barricades were up there was a great sense of euphoria; this was perhaps naive but it was nonetheless real. When the IRA campaign began the civil rights campaign was still going on, albeit on a smaller scale than previously, and the honeymoon period immediately after the arrival of the British troops was over. For the first time in the 6 counties one had the combination of armed struggle and mass, popular struggle. Most of the Catholics had withdrawn from the institutions of state and when internment came they all withdrew. The armed struggle began to be waged with great intensity and with major support and tolerance. There was also the feeling that things were happening in Dublin, as reflected in the Arms Trial crisis in Fianna Fáil, and that tended to give Northern Catholics succour.

When Prime Minister Faulkner said things like 'We have them on the run' and the IRA came back the next day with a devastating series of operations, the effect that had in lifting people's morale was enormous. The free run for republicans in the barricaded areas meant that the areas were almost entirely free of petty crime, and this had more to do with an identification with the struggle than with any policing methods of republicans.

The ambassadors for the British government on a daily basis were the British soldiers. They were 'welcomed' initially because they were seen as relieving a siege, whether in the Falls Road or in Derry, but it was an uneasy welcome. They got tea in only a few households. People did not know whether to cheer or what to do. Even in the past when Catholics had joined the British army for lack of available jobs their families had been inclined to feel a bit guilty about it. At the very least there was a consciousness that these were British soldiers and that in one sense or another we were Irish. Another factor which came quickly into play was the racist attitude of many British army regiments. They antagonised whole communities by their behaviour and especially by their attitude to womenfolk. So, while there were initially mixed feelings about the British army, once it became apparent what their role was, then all ambiguity went out of the window. Within a very short space of time people were shouting insults at the soldiers — things like 'Dunkirk harriers', which I didn't even understand at the time and which was the most polite kind of comment; and people were suddenly talking about memories of the Black and Tans.

Bombay Street, and two months later Coates Street, were burned down by loyalist gangs and the RUC after the British troops had arrived and after the larger scale burnings had already taken place. Whole streets of houses were burned out, people were killed and about a hundred injured during the two-day attack on this Catholic area in the Lower Falls. The fact that the British army did not intervene taught nationalists an important lesson.

The Falls Road curfew in July 1970 made popular opposition to the British army absolute in Belfast. Three thousand British troops invaded the Falls Road and from helicopters voices over PA systems announced that the area was under a curfew: anyone on the streets was liable to be shot. Five civilians were killed, more were injured, and three hundred were arrested. The invasion and curfew lasted for two days, during which 1,600 cannisters of CS gas were fired. Troops smashed down the doors of houses, pulled up floors, wrecked people's homes. The siege was broken, at great risk to themselves, by hundreds of women who massed together and simply marched past all the squaddies, who did not know how to cope with this direct expression of popular feeling. After that recruitment to the IRA was massive. IRA organisation and capability increased so dramatically that by June and July of 1971 they were able to carry out as many as 125 bombings in those two months — an average of more than two per day. The Stormont government and the British army were not succeeding in their attempts to crush the resistance.

The shooting dead in Derry of Seamus Cusack and Desmond Beattie marked a critical turning point. Prime Minister Faulkner had in May given the British army carte blanche to fire on anyone acting 'suspiciously'; on 8 July 1971 they obliged and two unarmed Catholics were killed. The struggle for civil rights had continued despite the RUC beating people to death, despite loyalist attacks, despite the Battle of the Bogside, the upheavals of August, the shootings of people in the Falls Road. But the shootings of Cusack and Beattie marked a change and this change was cemented by the use of the British army forces as the implement of repression. Before that it had been primarily a battle between beleagured nationalists and the Stormont administration for equal rights; then it became a battle between beleagured nationalists and the British establishment.

The British government could have defused the situation, could have prevented it reaching the stage of open armed conflict. If they had understood and taken note of what the Campaign for Social Justice was saying in 1965 they could have moved then to introduce the norms of democracy at a time when republicanism was virtually dead. In such circumstances it would have been impossible for the IRA to survive. If in London the will had existed to make even limited changes the long-sighted agitators would have pointed out how small the changes were and how unsatisfactory, but the British government would have succeeded in undercutting support for republicanism.

Instead of defusing the situation the British government copper-fastened popular support for the IRA. In Ballymurphy in West Belfast, for example, there were six semi-active republicans and ten supporters in 1969; today in West Belfast Sinn Féin draws its biggest vote from that area. The crucial transformation came about when a British army regiment came into Ballymurphy and attempted to beat its people into submission. If they had come in with kid gloves they would still have been unwelcome but they would not have generated the same phenomenon of implacable republican resistance.

Internment, introduced on 9 August 1971, had a major effect in making people conscious participants in the struggle. Those who were already politicised were not surprised by the introduction of internment, but there were many Catholics who did not believe that such a thing could happen, and to them internment came as a crucial indication that the road to reform was blocked off. Brutal confirmation came with the shooting dead of unarmed demonstrators in Derry on Bloody Sunday, 30 January 1972. Óglaigh na hÉireann was inundated with new recruits.

When Stormont fell in March 1972 it was a time of complete and utter jubilation. I remember talking to a middle-aged man in Ballymurphy in the midst of a collossal gun battle. (Although many people might not realise this, a lot of those big gun battles fought to defend an area from attack — in this case attack by the British army — had as many as two hundred people standing and watching what was happening.) This man, who had lived through the imposition of partition and the setting up of Stormont, kept saying, almost as if he was drunk, 'Jesus, you'd never think you'd see the day!' He represented a feeling that so quickly after the events of 1968/69 something that was hated, something that was symbolic of all that was wrong in the state had been removed. And probably most people who were anti-Unionist felt quite rightly that they had played a part in the removal of Stormont. The IRA was clearly seen as acting on their behalf.

The fall of Stormont was very decidedly a watershed. The feeling was that 'we'll never go back to that again'. Today there is a section of the population, represented by the SDLP, who will be prepared to go back. And there is a section who will never again accept partitionist rule. The respective strengths of those two tendencies remain to be seen.

The impact of the fall of Stormont on the Unionists, as well as the disarming and disbanding of the 'B' Specials, must obviously have been catastrophic. Having said that, the actual impact may have been exaggerated by commentators. Just after the fall of Stormont I found myself committed to the Maidstone prison ship, which was anchored in Belfast Lough in the hinterland of loyalist East Belfast and we felt very vulnerable to attack by an Orange mob enraged at the abolition of their Protestant parliament. The Vanguard Party was in its heyday, with its parades and rallies featuring fascist salutes. Unionist leaders were making threatening noises, and if there was going to be a real Orange backlash that was the moment at which it should have occurred. But it didn't; and in assessing the dangers of a loyalist backlash one must take this into account. They said they would not accept the fall of Stormont, but they did; they said they would fight to the last man, but they didn't.

What loyalist response there was came in a form which has been seen on many other occasions since. Although their fight over the proroguing of Stormont was with the British they engaged in a spiralling campaign of killings of Catholics. There was not the major backlash that had been threatened but there were the phenomena of multilated bodies and 'romper room' torture and it was a very frightening period for many Catholics, marked also by the growth to quite massive numbers of the UDA, which paraded in paramilitary gear and masks. There was also a major confrontation between the UDA and the British army in Woodvale in Belfast. The British army climbed down.

Unionism had depended for so long on its leadership that when that leadership failed to deliver Unionism was for a period lost — not only because its leadership had proved inadequate but also because the British government on whom it depended, to which it pledged allegiance, to which it felt bound and of which it was a subject took away Stormont. Their disarray became exacerbated when the British under direct rule took more and more of the everyday decisions and there was no real role for Unionist politicians. They had no power.

On the nationalist side Óglaigh na hÉireann enjoyed credibility and popular support but the republican movement failed to intervene politically and effectively handed over the role of political representatives of the nationalist people to the SDLP. Many Catholics adopted a pragmatic attitude then of support for the IRA's military struggle and voting for the SDLP. Some elements claiming to be 'republican' or 'nationalist' made attacks on Protestants. These attacks were quite wrong and, like 'feuding' between republican and other groups, did not serve any anti-Unionist interest.

Support for the IRA amongst the nationalist population of the 6 counties has been, as the tacticians of guerrilla warfare such as Mao and Che put it, the sea in which the people's army has swum and, like the sea, it has its tides, its ebbs and flows, but it is always there. The nationalist people had withdrawn their consent to being governed by Stormont; they and the IRA had brought Stormont down and proceeded in succeeding years to make the 6 counties ungovernable even in an environment of British military saturation of nationalist areas. However, a situation of deadlock in which Óglaigh na hÉireann were able to block the imposition of a British solution but were unable to force the British to withdraw produced a sense of war-weariness. The IRA had succeeded in bring down Stormont and they had promised victory in the form of British withdrawal. But victory had not come and the troops were still on the streets, still kicking down doors in the night, wrecking nationalists' houses, dragging people off for interrogation, torture and internment. British army patrols were sometimes truculent, sometimes terrified, but they were always there; whether you were going shopping or to work, to the pub or just round the corner to a relative or friend, they were always there. And that operated in many ways: it made people determined to resist, and it made people weary. British soldiers harrassed children leaving schools; mothers went down to the schools to bring their children home and prevent them responding to the provocations of the soldiers with stones; mothers saw sons graduating from stones to petrol bombs to membership of the IRA, to Long Kesh internment camp. Hardly a family was untouched by death, internment or imprisonment.

Heroically they kept their households going, often holding down a job while husband and perhaps a son as well were inside, coping on the barest level of subsistence, visiting Long Kesh regularly. Some became political activists in the Relatives Action Committee or in Sinn Féin; they marched and demonstrated and came to be the heart and soul of popular resistance.

In the face of the suffering of the war of resistance in the nationalist ghettoes it was inevitable that a war-weary opposition to the IRA would surface on occasions. It may well be, as other observers and authors have suggested, that some of these movements of opposition received encouragement and finance from British government, including British army sources. However, there is no doubt that on occasions genuine war-weariness did surface, and it is very understandable that it should, but because it occasionally attacked the IRA did not mean that it was pro-British. The appalling disruption of everyday life, the incessant assault on nerves by the tension of wondering whether a son, daughter, wife, husband, brother or sister was going to be lifted, beaten up in interrogation, interned or killed, the frequent dangers of loyalist assassination campaigns — all the strains of the situation inevitably raised the question in people's minds as to whether it was all worth it. No one wanted to go back to the 'normality' of rule by Stormont, but with no immediate prospect of a British withdrawal support for the struggle of the IRA was bound to waver. In particular, the British government exploited every opportunity to increase the sense of war-weariness; and especially when Óglaigh na hÉireann killed or injured civilians the British were always, in classical counter-insurgency fashion, cynically prepared to exploit these mistakes or to create the conditions in which they might occur.

There always has been and there always will be a yearning for peace among Irish people. The so-called 'Peace People' are the best-known example of an organised movement against the IRA campaign, but there have been other organisations through the years such as 'Women Together' and 'Protestant and Catholic Encounter', and there have been occasions when people in nationalist areas have protested against IRA actions without actually forming any organisation. But whenever this understandable and undoubtedly genuine desire for peace manifests itself it is open to exploitation for one political purpose or another. It is easy to suggest that peace is somehow not political and that peace marches are not political, and then sincere people can be swept along behind a vague and emotional demand.

I have very strong personal feelings about the 'Peace People' campaign of 1976. The IRA man, Danny Lennon, who was shot dead in the incident which gave rise to the campaign, had been a particular friend of mine since we had met in Cage 11 in Long Kesh. It was tragic enough that he and the Maguire children had been killed, but when the British lie about his death was picked up by the media and gained general acceptance I found it a great deal more difficult to deal with.

The facts of the incident were that Danny Lennon was shot dead at the wheel of the car he was driving by British soldiers firing from an armour-plated landrover and the car ploughed into the Maguire family at the side of the road. Mrs Maguire was seriously injured and three of her children, the oldest of whom was eight years and the youngest only six weeks, were killed. It was never clear whether they were killed by the car or by bullets fired by British soldiers; unusually, the results of the autopsies and inquest were never published.

No attention was focussed on the fact that the British troops had opened fire on a car without regard for the lives of civilians on the street. Instead, the headlines shouted their message that an IRA car had killed three children. And on BBC TV News that night Mrs Maguire's sister, Mairead Corrigan, broke down crying and understandably affected millions of viewers deeply.

Danny Lennon had been shot dead, yet he was being held solely responsible for the deaths of the Maguire children. It was bad enough that innocent children had been killed. That was awful. But Danny Lennon, now dead and unable to defend himself, was being blamed. That concern may appear ridiculous to people who have an image of IRA volunteers as terrorists, but the reality is that members of Óglaigh na hÉireann are just ordinary citizens who are forced through difficult circumstances into resistance, and Danny Lennon was an ordinary nationalist youth, a member of a large family in Andersonstown, who had become involved in resistance. The tragedy of the deaths of the children rankled; in particular, the way the British escaped any responsibility at all; the exploitation of the childrens' deaths; the cynical way in which the incident was manipulated.

The 'Peace People' lost credibility in nationalist areas very quickly. In fact, what credibility it had consisted basically of sympathy for the Maguires and, indeed, for the Lennons. Only four days after the deaths of the Maguire children a 12 year-old girl, Majella O'Hare, was shot and killed by British soldiers in South Armagh; the 'Peace People' offered no criticism of the British army. Two months later 14 year-old Brian Stewart was shot dead by British soldiers in West Belfast; again the 'Peace People' were silent, and when they went to a meeting in Turf Lodge they had to be escorted from the hall because of the fury of local people at the one-sidedness of their condemnation of violence. If that was not enough to seal their fate in Catholic areas they put the cap on it when they characterised the RUC, UDR and British army as 'the only legitimate upholders of the rule of law' and played down what they called 'the occasional instances when members of the security forces may have stepped beyond the rule of law'.

The movement showed that there is always a hope among people that there can be peace, an element of war-weariness that grabs at straws. The people who marched and prayed and engaged in rallies were expressing perfectly reasonable emotions, but these emotions were exploited. The 'Peace People' were not even calling for real and general peace: what they were calling for was an end to the armed struggle of the IRA. And that was at best a partial kind of peace, in both meanings of partial — prejudiced against only one element in a violent conflict and incomplete in that it did not base itself on the elements of social justice without which peace simply cannot grow. It was an attempt to move people away from republican physical force politics and it failed because it did not even seek to remedy the reasons why people felt compelled to have recourse to physical force.

As soon as they tried to examine what peace was and how it could be atained the leadership of the 'Peace People' began to collapse. The media, perhaps because of their nature, represent the failure as lying in the falling out between Mairead Corrigan, Betty Williams and Ciaran McKeown as they disputed who should get what money. But the real reason was far larger than this merely symptomatic disintegration. Peace rallies and prayer may give succour to people but they cannot of their own volition bring peace. Peace is a political question and cannot be successfully approached without a commitment to political change.

For a short period the 'Peace People' succeeded in diverting public — and particularly international — attention from the real problem of the political situation in the 6 counties. In the end it brought into question the credibility not only of its own leaders but also of the Nobel Peace Prize, Joan Baez, and others who associated themselves with it.

The episode — for that is what it was — of the 'Peace People' deserves to be regarded as a particularly sad one, because it represented a perversion of what is a very important demand. In practice, people have been demanding peace since long before the IRA became active. In my own area of Ballymurphy community groups have long demanded employment, decent housing, play centres, facilities for the aged, the handicapped and the young. They have sought freedom from heavy rents on homes they will never own, freedom from the dole queues and freedom from the Assistance Office. At the time of the 'Peace People' the facilities of the area were a public house, a row of shops, a bookmaker's office. One hundred of the six hundred families had more than ten people living in cramped, ill-repaired, misplanned, jerrybuilt houses. Forty-seven per cent of the residents were unemployed. Sixty per cent of the population were children and teenagers faced with a future which offered them nothing. Those demands for the kind of peace which is based on justice and equality were made year after year, and year after year they were refused.

We cannot have justice and peace in Ireland because we do not have a society capable of upholding them. Instead we have a system based on coercion, violence, sectarianism and exploitation. By its very nature British rule cannot be just or peaceful and, while this is so, revolutionary struggle will continue to strive to overthrow it in pursuit of true justice, peace and happiness. Violence in Ireland has its roots in the conquest of Ireland by Britain. This conquest has lasted through several stages for many centuries and, whether economic, political, territorial or cultural, it has used violence, coercion, sectarianism and terrorism as its methods and has had power as its objective.

*　　*　　*

While the armed struggle has traditionally dominated republican strategy, in this phase it has involved and depended upon a considerable degree of political support. IRA members do not go to people who provide support without being receptive to their thoughts. They do not constantly ask people to do things for them without being responsive to their needs, being careful about how they deal with them, and taking on board some of the criticisms they might have of aspects of the armed struggle. Not only is that receptiveness and responsiveness correct in political terms, it is also a practical necessity in everyday circumstances. If a person providing support is offended by the actions of Óglaigh na hÉireann then that person will withdraw their support and it will not be possible to continue with the armed activity as before.

Aspects of the nature of the armed struggle can be explored by comparing the British soldier and the IRA volunteer. The British soldier is brought to Ireland: he has all his equipment handed to him, he is put into a garrison, given his transport and pointed at whatever task it is that he has to perform. IRA volunteers first of all have to obtain weapons: these may be given to them by higher command or they may have to procure them themselves. They then have to arrange to be able to dump those weapons, and to do this they have to enlist someone's support. If they are on the run they have to arrange billets for themselves, they have to go and ask someone if they can stay in their house. They have no meal tickets: someone has to agree to feed them. And if they want to get from A to B they have to get someone to agree to provide transport.

To get through a normal day an active IRA volunteer is all the time involved in politics, all the time enlisting support, going to people and asking them to do this and that for him or her. Even if one could describe the armed struggle of Óglaigh na hÉireann as militaristic it bears little resemblance to what may be called militarism in terms of a standing army. Despite all the British progaganda stories it is obvious that the IRA exists and operates with the active consent of a sufficient number of people to finance, arm, clothe, feed, accommodate and transport IRA volunteers and in every way build up around them a voluntary political infrastructure.

The armed struggle requires the development of reflex physical force politics. Even if there were no unarmed political struggle, the armed struggle itself has a significant political dimension to it and involves a significant political relationship with the community. As volunteers develop their politics, their vision of the goal they are aiming for, as they come to understand the politics of their opponents and the way the struggle needs to develop, then comes an understanding that armed struggle itself is a tactic and that one cannot shoot or bomb an independent Ireland into existence. You may be able to bomb and shoot a British connection out of existence, given many other necessary political conditions, but you will not bring anything into existence.

The tactic of armed struggle is of primary importance because it provides a vital cutting edge. Without it the issue of Ireland would not even be an issue. So, in effect, the armed struggle becomes armed propaganda. There has not been, at least not yet, a classic development from guerilla action to mass military action registering territorial gains; instead, armed struggle has become an agent of bringing about change. That reality is understood even by middle-class professional people, people who have a stake in the 6 counties. Very many people who disagree absolutely with the IRA nevertheless see it as a very important part of the political equation. They might deplore it, dislike it, have moral objections to it, but still have the feeling that if it did not exist there would be no hope of getting change. At the same time there is a realisation in republican circles that armed struggle on its own is inadequate and that non-armed forms of political struggle are at least as important political struggle are at least as important. As a means of struggle against the British presence in the 6 counties in pursuance of national independence, armed action represents a necessary form of struggle; it has, however, no role to play in the 26 counties. The struggle there must be non-armed, complimentary to the struggle in the 6 counties and aimed also at securing national independence.

There are considerable moral problems in relation to armed struggle. I cannot conceive of any thinking person who would not have scruples about inflicting any form of hurt on another living being. The republican carrying out an armed action might be very ruthless, determined and callous, but intellectually and emotionally he or she would have difficulty. That difficulty would rarely lie in any sense of religious morality but would have to do with the type of struggle involved, because it is close-up and it is nothing like joining a 'regular' army with a whole ethos about being trained to kill. IRA volunteers are actually civilians, political people who decide for short periods in their lives to take part in armed action. That is different from somebody who wants to join a 'regular' army, who wants to be a good shot, who wants a military career. The reality is of people who have consciously decided that armed struggle is a political necessity and that they will, in a fairly haphazard way, train themselves in the rudiments of military capability. There are no careerists in the IRA. Republican volunteers face futures of suffering, imprisonment and death.

What gives many people a problem is the length of the struggle. Even ordinary people who feel reservations might not have the same reservations if they felt it was going to be over in a short space of time — a two- or three-year war after which you start building right away. And it is worth pointing out what has happened in other, analagous situations, that the revolutionaries become the best builders; apart from their political commitment, perhaps because of their previous involvement in the destruction of other human beings.

The morality of the establishment does not concern me at all. It is a case — to borrow a phrase from Seamus Deane's *Civilians and Barbarians* — of a political code disguised as a moral code. I hear Garret FitzGerald saying that he will not talk to those who will not renounce violence, and then he goes to meet Margaret Thatcher, who is up to her neck in the use of armed force in Ireland and other parts of the world. No republican would have the brass neck to express such blatant double standards.

Obviously I would prefer a situation where armed struggle was unnecessary or even where armed struggle could be limited completely to what one could awkwardly call 'clean' operations, where you had Óglaigh na hÉireann and the British army shooting it out. I do not mean 'shooting it out' in some kind of heroic sense. The odds are stacked against the IRA volunteers and they operate at great personal risk against forces which are numerically and technologically superior and much better equipped. I admire the tenacity, determination and self-sacrifice of IRA volunteers but I do not think that any war should be glamourised. In the 6 counties armed struggle is a terrible but necessary form of resistance which is engaged in as a means towards an independent Ireland. The assessement in November 1978 by Brigadier J.M. Glover of British army intelligence concluded that while the British army remained in Ireland the IRA would remain in existence to fight them. Most impartial observers and many opponents of republicanism recognise that the British presence is the catalyst for the armed struggle.

There are no material benefits for volunteers. Even a *Sunday Tribune* investigation had to conclude that they could find no evidence of republicans making material gains from their involvement. If the life of an IRA volunteer was a career one might be able to talk about people who wanted to keep the war going rather than lose their livelihoods, but there is not even that mercenary element. War is also a very draining process. We who are republicans, whether militarily involved or not, at least have a choice — nobody, after all, forced us to become involved — but it still becomes extremely draining. At some time we are going to have to get on with our own lives and pursue our own private ambitions. After all the years of struggle I look at the city of Belfast which I admire so much and I feel sick about the way in which it has been turned upside down and I regret that people throughout the course of this war have suffered so much in so many different ways.

A repeated assertion by the Dublin government and some other elements opposed to us is that because republicans are engaged in armed action now they would continue to use armed action in an independent Ireland. What I think they are really saying is that an independent Ireland poses a threat to them, that getting rid of partition means opening a Pandora's box. They are threatened by the spectre of the working people, Protestant and Catholic, no longer divided by partition or sectarian privilege and as a majority galvanising their political position. They are threatened by the notion of normal class politics developing in an independent Ireland invigorated and encouraged by an immense feeling of euphoria after the settlement of this long war. And the only people who are threatened by that are those who have a vested interest in maintaining the status quo. These, then, are the people who are loudest in their condemnation of the armed struggle and who nowadays hold up the prospect that the republicans are going to come over the border and visit violence upon the 26 counties. This is not going to happen.

I meet members of the public constantly in the 26 counties. I cannot be anywhere in a public place or even walk down the street without people coming over and telling me what they think. Their main concern in relation to the IRA is that the war is going on so long. Some have a particular political attitude, in that they would like to see the British out, some are concerned about the loyalists and the difficulty posed by the strength of loyalism. But in all my fairly widespread travels in the 26 counties the worry about the IRA being habituated to violence has not been expressed.

Even if one looks at the matter from a purely tactical point of view, the ingredients for armed struggle are inherent in the 6 county state. But following the restoration of Irish national independence there would be no popular support for armed struggle. The handful of people who make up Óglaigh na hÉireann could not hope to win anything by pursuing armed struggle without popular support. In its origins and in its continuing role the modern IRA is an almost entirely working class organisation of political militants which enjoys popular support amongst nationalists in the cities, towns and countryside of the 6 counties and a degree of passive support in the 26 counties. British Army Brigadier J.M. Glover was forced to conclude that:

> Our evidence of the calibre of rank and file terrorists (sic) does not support the view that they are merely mindless hooligans drawn from the unemployed and unemployable.

A study by lawyers of defendants appearing before the Diplock (non-jury) courts charged with 'scheduled' offences produces another outsiders' view of IRA volunteers (though by no means all of those charged before the courts were IRA members or even republican activists):

> We are satisfied that the data establishes beyond reasonable doubt that the bulk of the republican offenders are young men and women without criminal records in the ordinary sense, though some have been involved in public disorders of the kind that frequently took place in the areas in which they liv-

ed. Both in this respect and in other records of employment and unemployment, they are reasonably representative of the working-class community of which they form a substantial part . . . They do not fit the stereotype of criminality which the authorities have from time to time attempted to attach to them.

It seems strange to reproduce such sociological comment upon my comrades of the republican movement, but I am aware that there may be readers of this book who are habitual consumers of the British press, the 6 counties press or the 26 counties press and who are habitual listeners to or viewers of British or Irish television and radio. Given the constant stream of lies which have spewed out over the years not just from the British and Dublin governments but also from the media, it may be useful to show that even lawyers and a senior figure in British military intelligence are forced to recognise that the IRA are neither hooligans nor criminals.

I find it ridiculous to have to make the points I have just made, because they have nothing to do with reality; they have instead to do with a crude propaganda war. The very people who originate the propaganda lines that wind up as press headlines know perfectly well that the IRA is not a matter of 'godfathers of crime', of 'pathological killers', of 'mad bombers', of 'mindless hooligans'; they know that in dealing with the IRA they are dealing with determined political opponents who are using the only means at their disposal to bring home their message in terms that will be understood and taken seriously enough to result in action and movement.

An example today of how far the British government is prepared to go to break republican resistance can be found in their efforts to dehumanise women republican prisoners by the brutal means of forced strip-searching. It is an indication of the courage and resilience of these women that after years of being subjected, sometimes on a daily basis, to this brutal, degrading and inhuman treatment, the women remain unbowed and unbroken. Similarly, there is the plight of long-term prisoners, especially the young prisoners, serving unprecedented sentences at the whim of a British judge or a British government minister. Many of these prisoners started their sentences as juveniles and are now in their thirties. Others were young married men and are now grandfathers. This experience has obviously traumatised their families and it is a miracle of human endurance and a credit especially to the wives and mothers that their families have survived. It is also remarkable that so many released prisoners return to the struggle, and it is an indication of the durability of resistance that there is still an active struggle to embrace them after ten, twelve or thirteen years of imprisonment.

The IRA has maintained its struggle against massive odds. Its members have been interned, imprisoned without trial, shot down in cold blood. The areas in which it operates have been subjected to all the devices of social control that multi-million pound investment in the modern technology of repression can muster. The IRA is ordinary people facing up against the monster of imperial power, and I have no reservation whatsoever in saluting those who have made it impossible for the British army and government to succeed, despite their massive firepower, in imposing their imperial will.

Political Status

If you strike at, imprison or kill us,
Out of our prisons or graves
We will still evoke a spirit that will thwart you,
And, mayhap, raise a force that will destroy you.
   We defy you! Do your worst.
                              James Connolly, December 1914

THE MOST SUSTAINED British propaganda campaign against the IRA was organised against the background of a protracted cessation of IRA activity around the attempt to portray the IRA as 'common criminals'. Abolishing political status for prisoners charged with 'scheduled' (i.e. war-related) offenses, the British engaged in an intense and energetic campaign of psychological warfare, or 'psy-ops'. Press releases, speeches and statements from the administration referred consistently to republican leaders as 'godfathers' and suchlike. Stories of corruption and gangsterism in the republican movement were invented and judiciously placed in Fleet Street. The advent of the 'Peace People' in August of the same year was well-timed to add substantially to the British propaganda effort.

In the nationalist ghettoes popular mobilisations were at an all-time low and the prevailing atmosphere was one of war-weariness. Sinn Féin, its ability to organise constantly undermined by arrests, harrassment and imprisonment, was a small protest organisation and support group for the IRA and was only experiencing the first stirrings of a feeling that it needed to develop itself as a political organisation capable of intervening and mobilising on a range of issues. The Relatives Action Committee, comprising almost exclusively women from the ghettoes of nationalist West Belfast, stood outside the republican movement and had only a limited capacity to mobilise support for the prisoners. The policy of 'criminalisation' struck at the heart of the republican struggle, and it did so at a time when it was politically weak. The resilience of nationalist resistance and the central question of support for the IRA were to be tested over the six years from 1976 to 1981 as never before.

The republican insistence on the importance of political prisoner status has nothing to do with any contempt for the 'ordinary criminals' who are so often the victims of social inequality and injustice. From Thomas Ashe to Bobby Sands the concern has always been to assert the political nature of the struggle in which the IRA has been engaged. In September 1917 eighty-four republican prisoners went on hunger strike for political status; one of them, Thomas Ashe, leader of the Irish Republican Brotherhood, died after force feeding; political status was granted then by the British authorities and Ashe's death proved a turning point in rallying mass support behind the demand for independence.

British governments have from time to time granted and withdrawn political status. In June 1972 a hunger strike in Crumlin Road prison in Belfast led by Billy McKee resulted in the recognition of political status, but in January 1975 a government-appointed committee under Lord Gardner called for its abolition. Harold Wilson's Labour government announced that anyone arrested after 1 March 1976 was to be regarded as a criminal without political status. In resisting this move republicans were asserting the political nature of their struggle and contradicting the British attempt to suggest to the world that the political crisis in the 6 counties was not a political crisis at all but was merely a problem with criminal elements.

The contradictions in the British position were enormous but their access to world media and the resources they could bring to bear in the propaganda war meant that they could achieve considerable success in presenting the struggle in the 6 counties as a species of 'Mafia terrorism'. When the contradictions threatened to emerge they used various means in their continuing psy-ops war to obscure the reality of the situation. And the reality was that special laws has been enacted to counter the armed struggle of the IRA; the law was being used, to repeat Brigadier Kitson's phrase, as 'just another weapon in the government's arsenal . . . a propaganda cover'. Special courts had been established, known as the Diplock courts, to deprive those accused of 'special category' or 'scheduled' offenses of trial by jury. Special concentration camps had been constructed to house those convicted of special category offences as well as those interned without trial. To turn around then and deny that these were special category prisoners was to fly in the face of logic and reality.

An essential element in Britain's criminalisation strategy was the conveyor-belt system of — to use Kitson's phrase again — 'disposal of unwanted members of the public'. Juryless courts were not sufficient to secure guaranteed convictions of republicans, but the systematic use of torture, primarily carried out in the purpose-built interrogation centre at Castlereagh in Belfast, ensured that detainees could be forced to sign incriminating statements. Once anyone had signed a statement it was only a matter of passing them on to the next stage of the conveyor-belt where British judges did the job they were paid for and processed them on to the final stage, the H-Blocks of Long Kesh or the Women's Prison in Armagh.

Republicans faced an uphill battle in trying to reverse the tide of British government propaganda. Even when the facts indicated to any competent journalist that wholesale torture was producing litanies of dubious confessions the media were determined to avoid reporting anything which might seem to support the repubican position. However, when in June 1978 Amnesty International called for a public inquiry into the 'maltreatment' practised at Castlereagh, the media were at last prepared to admit that something was going on and the first chink appeared in Britain's propaganda war. Giving just 78 cases of maltreatment of suspects, and estimating that between 70 per cent and 90 per cent of Diplock court convictions were achieved on the sole or main basis of self-incriminating statements, the Amnesty report was far from comprehensive and failed to document the extent and intensity of the torture policy. However, weak as it was, the Amnesty report posed enough of a threat to Britain's psy-ops for the Independent Broadcasting Authority (IBA) to step in and ban a television programme on it. Later in the same year Fr Raymond Murray and Fr Denis Faul published a far more extensive report on Castlereagh. Fr Faul is in the habit of making vitriolic attacks on republicans and receives considerable media attention for these attacks; on the other hand, his and Fr Murray's collations of British brutality, such as their file on Castlereagh, have been either ignored or received with hostility by the media.

However, the success of this British strategy began to falter when a police surgeon, Dr Robert Irwin, came forward to state that he had personal knowledge of at least 150 people who had been seriously injured in RUC custody at Castlereagh. Even Independent Television News could not ignore such authoritative evidence, and the British government were faced with a problem. The busy beavers of the British army intelligence psy-ops department quickly spread rumours designed to destroy the doctor's credibility, alleging that he was seeking revenge for his wife's rape by a British soldier. The government also rushed out a report, the Bennett Report, which offered the mildest of rebukes to those engaged in the torture in Castlereagh. However, the British had suffered a setback in their propaganda war and it was probably at this time that they began to lay plans for the use of paid informers to secure convictions.

Attention switched to the H-Blocks of Long Kesh where republican prisoners developed their own opposition to British policy. Prisoners required under the new conditions after 1 March 1976 to wear prison uniform rejected this badge of criminalisation and, not permitted to wear their own clothing, wore blankets instead. The republican attitude was well captured in Francie Brolly's song:

I'll wear no convict's uniform
Nor meekly serve my time
That England might
Brand Ireland's fight
800 years of crime.

Kieran Nugent, the first person to be sentenced for a 'scheduled offense' after the arbitrarily chosen date, was the first to refuse, on 14 September 1976, to wear prison clothing. 'If they want me to wear a convict's uniform,' he said, 'they'll have to nail it to my back.'

Parallel with their withdrawal of political status the British government stepped up their propaganda campaign to portray the IRA as 'godfathers of terrorism' manipulating naive teenagers into committing robberies so that these same 'godfathers' could live in luxury houses and drive luxury cars. In particular they successfully promoted to sections of the British media the image of Maire Drumm, Vice-President of Sinn Féin, as a 'godmother of terrorism' and 'grandmother of hate'. She was shot dead in bed at the Mater Hospital in Belfast where she was being treated for cataracts.

Prison warders subjected the 'blanket men' to constant harassment. In 1978 they attacked prisoners as they went to and from the latrines, kicked over chamber pots in cells and threw the contents of pots onto beds. The prisoners were forced to respond by escalating the 'blanket' protest to a 'no wash' stage; they refused to shave, wash or empty chamber pots. Conditions rapidly became appalling.

Cardinal Tomás Ó Fiaich visited the H-Blocks in August 1978 and gave the following description:

> One could hardly allow an animal to remain in such conditions, let alone a human being. The nearest approach to it that I have ever seen was the spectacle of hundreds of homeless people living in the sewer pipes of the slums of Calcutta. The stench and the filth in some of the cells with the remains of rotten food and human excreta scattered around the walls was almost unbearable.

At the time the prison authorities, the government and the media portrayed the 'no wash' protest as arising simply from a conscious decision by the prisoners. However, I was brought to Long Kesh, held on remand on a charge of IRA membership, and discovered for myself how the provocation by the prison officers had brought the situation about.

Relatives — almost all women — of prisoners had in late April 1976 set up the Relatives Action Commitee to campaign for the restoration of political status. However, within Sinn Féin we lacked a structured national political response to the prison crisis. This began to change after the 1978 Sinn Fein Ard Fheis, at which Ruairi O Bradaigh, then President of Sinn Féin, drew attention to the true nature of the situation and signposted it as a priority for the movement. From that point on we attempted to build support on the outside for the protest of the prisoners.

The Relatives Action Committee, which was campaigning energetically, was a Belfast-based organisation and while we related to it locally we were unable to take a national approach to it. But, recognising our considerable shortcomings in dealing with the question, we held a national conference on the prison issue in 1979, a conference which involved the whole membership in detailed consideration. It was the first time that Sinn Féin had actually sat down and looked at a single issue, analysed it, discussed it and then embarked on spreading the knowledge shared and the conclusions come to, and it marked an important development for us.

We set about creating a proper POW department, which until then had been simply a service for the prisoners, and we began to look at the issue in terms of a political campaign. We produced pamphlets and leaflets and we began to seek ways to broaden out the campaign to involve other forces apart from our own members.

The creation of the H-Block/Armagh Committee as a united front was a very important element of the hunger strike. In 1978 we made a mistake in our approach to a conference called to discuss the building of a broad anti-Unionist front. Lack of experience and lack of preparation on our part resulted in this Coalisland conference becoming a lost opportunity to build unity, because the price our representatives asked for that unity was that all within the front should express support for the armed struggle of the IRA. It was a price that many of those who wished to unite in anti-Unionist action were not prepared to pay. One of the problems we suffered from at that time was that we were still emerging from a basically conspiratorial type of organisation. Also, we suffered from the effects of a high rate of attrition: members who had been involved in earlier united action with the Political Hostages Release Committee (1973-74) may well have learned lessons from it, but many or most of them were in jail or for the other reasons were not involved in our intervention in the Coalisland conference.

Sinn Féin was a protest movement and a movement of support for the IRA; it was at that time only just beginning to discuss strategy and tactics, to assess what our attitudes should be in any given circumstances. Part of the impact of our conspiratorial background was that we were temperamentally and organisationally disinclined to engage in any form of action with elements outside the movement itself. The movement had its origins in armed struggle, which had dominated to the extent of even being considered the only form of struggle; in such circumstances conspiratorial methods were, of course, essential. But what we were slowly and unevenly realising was that one could not build a political intervention on the basis of conspiratorial methods and approaches.

The IRA was constantly being denounced from all quarters and all standpoints. It was understandable that members of the movement had considerable difficulty in accepting the right of people with whom they were involved in joint action to attack the IRA. Members were increasingly coming into contact with organisations that expressed a position of 'critical support' for the IRA, and any republican was bound to feel that one either supported the IRA or one did not; 'critical support' seemed a contradiction in terms and a dishonest one at that. It took a maturing process on the part of republicans to appreciate that a position of critical support was better than one of not supporting at all.

By October 1979 our attitude to united action had changed dramatically and we had dropped the insistence on support for the armed struggle. At a conference in the Green Briar Hotel in Andersonstown, organised by the Relatives Action Committee, the organisations which set up the H-Block/Armagh Committee included Sinn Féin, the Irish Republican Socialist Party (IRSP), People's Democracy (PD), the Trade Union Campaign Against Repression (TUCAR) and Women Against Imperialism (WAI). There were even representatives present from the 'Peace People'.

While we were making attempts to organise the political campaign the protest was continuing inside the prisons and the IRA for its part was carrying out a campaign of shooting prison officers, nine being killed in 1979. To the prisoners themselves it seemed that little headway was being made, and they began to suggest that they should instigate a hunger strike. Brendan Hughes and others wrote from Long Kesh pointing out that the protest had been going on for three years and suggested that while the older prisoners could take it, the length of the protest placed an intolerable burden on the young prisoners coming into the blocks. Eighteen and nineteen year-olds faced the prospect of spending ten years on the blanket and no wash protest. There was an almost parental concern on the part of the older prisoners. And they felt that the onus was on them to achieve a short-term resolution of the prison conflict. This they proposed to pursue by means of a hunger strike. We advised strongly against hunger strike and promised — perhaps somewhat rashly and naively — to achieve movement on the issue by intensifying our efforts on the outside.

Meanwhile, the crisis in the prisons intensified. In February 1980 male guards wrecked the calls of republican women prisoners at Armagh jail and beat up several of the women. Prisoners were allowed to wear their own clothes at Armagh and so there had been no 'blanket' protest, but now the women both responded to the attacks on them and joined the struggle of their male comrades by embarking on the 'no wash' protest. In March the British government extended the denial of political status to those prisoners who had been sentenced before 1 March 1976; there was no sign that the government was willing to take significant steps to defuse the crisis.

The H-Block/Armagh Committee worked hard to raise public consciousness and bring pressure to bear on the British government. Allied to this campaigning, we engaged in intense lobbying. But the H-Block/Armagh campaign was unable to force the British government into movement on the issue, and in October 1980 the prisoners decided to go on hunger strike. In Sinn Féin we felt we were in no position to stop them: a year previously we had said that we would sort it out and now they were saying to us, in the nicest possible way, that we had failed. So, we were under an obligation to support the hunger strike: we had tried our means, now the prisoners were going to try theirs.

In late October seven H-Block prisoners started a hunger strike; in late November they were joined by three women prisoners in Armagh; in December thirty more H-Block prisoners went on hunger strike. One of the seven weakened physically more rapidly than the rest; he was losing his sight and was on the verge of lapsing into a coma. The British government, despite taking a hard line of 'no concessions' in public, indicated that a compromise could be reached and that a document setting out details of a settlement would be presented to the prisoners if they came off hunger strike. The hunger strikers considered the condition of Sean McKenna, who was fast approaching death, and considered the indications of movement by the government. Sean McKenna was too ill to take part in their deliberations. On the fifty-third day of the strike, 18 December, they called off the protest. Later that day the British presented a document to the prisoners, but meanwhile they were presenting the world news with a story of surrender, without giving details of any compromise package. The women in Armagh refused to come off hunger strike until they were assured by us that the men had actually ended their fast.

The document did not represent the kind of settlement that the prisoners would have accepted after negotiations, but Sinn Féin tried very hard, with Bobby Sands who was O/C of the IRA in Long Kesh at the time, to work positively within the confines of this very ambiguous and undefined set of proposals. Had they possessed the political will the British government could creditably within the terms of their own document have found a basis for a step-by-step implementation of the prisoners' demands, but I presume that when they saw the decline in morale which followed the end of the hunger strike they decided to obstruct any form of movement within the prisons. Twenty prisoners tested the willingness of the government to implement changes by coming off the 'no wash' and blanket protest; relatives brought clothes to Long Kesh but on 20 January 1981 the prison authorities refused to distribute the clothes to the men. The prisoners drew their conclusions and one week later a group of them smashed up their cells. Preparation began immediately for a second hunger strike.

Through Bobby Sands the prisoners conveyed to the republican movement outside the prisons their absolute determination to embark on another hunger strike. In calm, reasoned correspondence they showed that coldly and clinically they had worked out in great detail exactly how it would proceed. From the outside we continued to advise the prisoners that their deaths would not necessarily achieve the improvements they sought. They could be dead without any advantages accruing either in terms of prison conditions or of the overall struggle. Also, we felt that the movement could not stand another defeated hunger strike. I wrote to Bobby Sands, 'Bobby, we are tactically, strategically, physically and morally opposed to a hunger strike.' But by the time we had gone through all the arguments in our correspondence I knew that Bobby Sands was going to die.

The prison conditions could have operated as a safety valve: a sophisticated British government could have defused the situation quite easily and avoided a confrontation between itself as unyielding colonial power and a group of defenceless political prisoners, which is how it largely came to be seen internationally. The first hunger strike having ended, they would not have been acting under duress if they had allowed for some new arrangements on the specifics of prison conditions. But as the prisoners pressed for a second hunger strike they knew that this time not only would some of them have to die but also that they were engaging in a fight with the British government which now went beyond the issue of prison conditions; they were pitching themselves, with the only weapons at their command, against the imperial power. As they faced the prospect of death they felt that the spectacle of their deaths in prison was going to be politically productive for the republican cause to which they were committed.

Hunger strike is unlike any other form of struggle. An IRA volunteer does not go out to get killed; if he gets killed it is because he makes a mistake or some other circumstance arises. But a hunger striker embarks on a process which from day one is designed to end in his death. However, when people contemplate their own deaths there can be no guarantee that all will go according to plan, no guarantee that they will go through with it to the end. It takes a very particular kind of person to go all the way, to resist the voices in his own head, the concern of friends and family, not to mention the pressures of the authorities, and it is extremely difficult to know, until one is staring death right in the face, whether one is that particular kind of person.

Our opposition in Sinn Féin to the hunger strike had to do partly with that difficulty, partly with the fact that close personal relationships existed between the prisoners themselves and between prisoners and republicans on the outside, and we all knew we were entering a period of intense anguish. But primarily we opposed it because we did not believe that it would succeed in moving the British government. It must also be said that in terms of the political priorities of the movement we did not want the hunger strike. We were just beginning our attempts to remedy the political underdevelopment of the movement, trying to develop the organisation, engaging in a gradual build-up of new forms of struggle and, in particular, we were working out our strategy in relation to elections. We were well aware that a hunger strike such as was proposed would demand exclusive attention, would, in effect, hijack the struggle, and this conflicted with our sense of the political priorities of the moment.

Bobby Sands started his hunger strike on 1 March 1981, the fifth anniversary of the phasing out of political status. A large demonstration marched down the Falls Road in support of Bobby Sands and the five demands of the prisoners:

★ the right to wear their own clothing at all times;
★ exemption from all forms of penal labour;
★ free association with each other at all hours;
★ the right to organise their own recreational and educational programmes;
★ full restoration of remission.

Francis Hughes joined Bobby on hunger strike on 15 March, Ray McCreesh and Patsy O'Hara a week later.

After the initial march in Belfast the campaign of support developed slowly; it was difficult to mobilise people after the demoralising effect of the first hunger strike and we struggled to organise even small-scale actions such as pickets. However, the calling of a by-election in Fermanagh/South Tyrone, where sitting MP Frank Maguire, an independent nationalist, had died suddenly provided an immediate and dynamic focus for the campaign.

Young and not so young Sinn Féin members had no experience of organising an electoral campaign but they had plenty of energy and commitment and they combined well with independent republicans in the constituency, with Bernadette MacAliskey and with big Joe Keohane — up from Kerry to canvass support. On 9 April Bobby Sands was elected Member of the Westminster Parliament with 30,492 votes. His victory exposed the lie that the hunger strikers — and by extension the IRA and the whole republican movement — had no popular support. The British campaign of 'criminalisation' which motivated their removal of political status had sought to portray republicans as 'godfathers' operating by intimidation and as isolated fanatics. Their propaganda had now been dramatically refuted and the election of Bobby Sands resounded internationally. For many in the British Labour movement it was their road to Damascus. It had a particular impact on British MPs simply because of the status that the parliament at Westminster enjoys: a man had been elected on a massive popular vote who was, according to their lights, a terrorist and a criminal who was offering the people nothing.

The election victory intensified international interest in the hunger strike and uplifted absolutely the confidence and morale of republicans. There was a feeling amongst some of our members and supporters that surely the British government must yield sufficiently to bring about an end to the hunger strike. We had been challenged for years to submit ourselves to the ballot box and now we had done so. We had demonstrated massive popular support in votes; the hunger strikers had shown immense and awesome determination; we had mobilised mass demonstrations. Yet, whether we played by their rules or not, the British government, as we had feared from the outset, showed no willingness to make concessions.

However, we began to receive a stream of envoys from the Dublin government whose message was that the British would concede. Charles J. Haughey, who had recently succeeded Jack Lynch as Taoiseach and leader of Fianna Fáil, wanted to hold a general election in the 26 counties, but the hunger strike brought a degree of instability, or at least of unpredictability, which he was at pains to avoid. The envoys were well-known people in public life and they conveyed a uniform conviction that Charles Haughey was about to secure a means of resolving the hunger strike. One of the phrases used more than once was 'You're pushing at an open door' — a phrase which seems almost to be his motto since he is said to have used it in discussions with Monsignor Horan over Knock airport and in negotations with Independent TD Tony Gregory in Dublin. All the time the message was that the British government were about to concede the five demands. Our approach, in consultation with the prisoners, was to say, 'Alright, we'll believe you, but could we have that in writing, please?' And it seemed that as soon as we said that all agreement collapsed, and to this day I do not know how genuinely those envoys believed in the message they brought to us.

In the midst of everything some light relief was afforded by a spokesperson for the Dublin government. He was on the phone to Owen Carron in our Belfast office, conveying the same line that Haughey's envoys had been repeating one after the other, only more so. I and a number of others were in the office at the time listening to the conversation, and we were saying to Owen to ask him this and ask him that. Eventually the government spokesperson outlined what he said was a very definite offer from the British government and Owen asked him if he would stand over that.

'No', replied the caller, 'as far as I am concerned I never had this conversation with you.'

'Well,' said Owen, 'you're trying to get this hunger strike stopped: there has to be something more substantial than that.'

'Tell him,' I said to Owen, 'that you have the conversation taped.'

Well, Owen did just that and the government spokesperson erupted with the most amazing tirade of bad language in which the politest epithet was 'fucking bastard'!

There was something perversely funny, too, about the on-off story of the elections in the 26 counties. Every time an overture was being made to us the Dublin media were reporting that an election was almost certain to be announced within days. And as the overtures faded into thin air the speculations and predictions about election dates were suddenly being dismissed in the media. The Fianna Fáil leadership understood, of course, the possible effect of the hunger strike and they were trying to get it defused in order to have a clear run in an electoral contest.

In the course of their efforts they placed great emphasis on the International Red Cross, an organisation that had already expressed its opposition to political status. Members of Bobby Sands's family were sent for with great urgency; as they travelled south they were met at Swords in north County Dublin by a garda escort and rushed in the early hours in fairly dramatic circumstances to see the Taoiseach. Enormous pressure was put on them: if the prisoners, it was said, would only see the Red Cross then the British would give in and Bobby Sands's life would be saved. After such intense pressure, and with great misgivings, Marcella Sands agreed that the Red Cross should see Bobby. But there was never any real substance in the Red Cross intervention, and they were certainly not a vehicle by means of which the five demands were going to be granted.

Margaret Thatcher maintained her inflexible approach and,

despite all the earnest assurances of their envoys, the Dublin government did nothing to shift her from it.

Bobby Sands died on 5 May 1981, the 66th day of his hunger strike.

This book is not the place to record my personal feelings about the death of this friend and comrade, nor about the deaths of the other hunger strikers. Even if I was able to express those feelings adequately, I am probably still too close to them to be able to reflect upon them in tranquility. I would not like to live through the awful experience of the hunger strike again. Scarcely a day goes by in which I do not think of the lads who died.

One hundred thousand people followed the funeral procession of Bobby Sands through West Belfast. It was an overwhelming outpouring of public grief and of identification with Bobby Sands and the IRA. Masked volunteers fired a ceremonial volley of shots over the coffin.

Francis Hughes died on 12 May.

On 19 May the IRA killed five British soldiers with a land mine in South Armagh.

Patsy O'Hara and Ray McCreesh died on 21 May.

On 23 May local elections took place in the 6 counties. Sinn Féin did not participate but two IRSP and two PD members stood and were elected to Belfast city council, in the process unceremoniously dumping Gerry Fitt from the seat he had occupied for 23 years. Fitt had publicly called on Thatcher not to concede the five demands; now the Conservative Party's favourite Irishman, his political life in Ireland was over.

The Dublin government called a general election for 11 June; the hunger strike continued. The National H-Block/Armagh Committee put up nine republican prisoners — four of them hunger strikers — as candidates.

The media were unanimous in writing off the chances of the prisoner candidates. Political correspondents and editors were so strongly prejudiced against the republican movement that they deserted whatever professional skills, experience and standards they may have possessed and indulged instead in an exercise in wishful thinking. They dismissed the prisoners' campaign as being insignificant and proceeded then to ignore it.

So, with no media coverage apart from curt dismissals and condemnations, the campaign had its problems, but we had always received hostile media attention and we knew that there was a layer of potential support which was not dependent for its views on the media mandarins. What posed a more substantial obstacle was the fact that the dominant concerns of voters were economic and social; it was only to be expected that they would cast their ballots according to which parties and candidates seemed to offer the best policies in terms of the matters that affected their everyday lives. Our campaign offered nothing but asked simply for support for the five demands of the prisoners in the 6 counties. The prisoners were in no position to be able to serve their constituents, so anyone voting for them would have to be content with the notion of not being represented in Leinster House — a consideration of particular significance in a state where politics is so dominated by clientilist concerns and approaches. The National H-Block/Armagh Committee had no base of constituency workers such as provided the foundation for the electoral campaigns of the political parties; in two weeks and without prior constituency work towards an election, campaigns had to be built up and carried out in nine constituencies.

In the event two prisoner candidates — Paddy Agnew and Kieran Doherty — were elected; a third, Joe McDonnell, was within 300 votes of being elected, and the nine together ran up a very respectable tally of 40,000 votes. It was a triumphant expression of popular support for the prisoners.

Despite the message of the elections, the new government headed by Garret FitzGerald refused, as had Haughey's government, to take the steps proposed by the National H-Block/Armagh Committee: to recall their ambassador from London; to expell the British ambassador from Dublin; end army and Garda collaboration with the RUC and British army. The intransigence of Margaret Thatcher was criticised but no measure was taken which might have caused her to modify her stance.

In late June the British parliament changed the rules of its own 'democracy' by passing what became known as the 'Sands Bill', which prevented convicted felons from standing for Westminster elections. They had long demanded that we submit to the ballot box. We had done so and had been spectacularly successful. Their response was to ignore the results, refuse to recognise the MP and the movement he represented, and to change the rules to prevent a similar candidate being elected again.

Our response was to stand Owen Carron, who had been Bobby's election agent, in the new by-election in Fermanagh/South Tyrone.

Joe McDonnell died on hunger strike on 8 July.

Martin Hurson died on 13 July.

Kevin Lynch died on 1 August.

Kieran Doherty, who had been elected to Leinster House, died on 2 August.

Tom McElwee died on 8 August.

Micky Devine died on 20 August.

On the same day Owen Carron was elected as MP for Fermanagh/South Tyrone, exceeding Bobby Sands's vote by 800.

On 3 October the six remaining hunger strikers ended their protest. In the meantime some of the hunger strikers had taken individual decisions to end their hunger strikes. Ten men had sacrificed their lives; massive popular support for their stand had been shown in demonstrations, funerals and elections; things would never be the same again.

No republican will ever attach the slightest shadow of blame to those hunger strikers who individually ended their fasts. What the ten who died had done was so extraordinary that one almost needs another language in order to convey it in all its awful reality. Catholic clergy intervened with the relatives of hunger strikers to encourage them to bring about an end to the fasts by requesting medical help. But even without their intervention it was inevitable that some hunger strikers would eventually pull back in the face of death. I have no regrets whatsoever that some came off their hunger strikes; my regrets are reserved for those who died. My anger is reserved for the government that could quite easily have reached an honourable compromise in the face of the ultimate in selfless dedication to a cause.

Following the end of the hunger strike adjustments in the prison regime along the lines of the five demands began to be implemented. In an unprecedented way the prisoners had insisted on being recognised as prisoners in a war of national liberation, and their identity as such had been accepted throughout the world. Britain had been seen internationally as an intransigent force clinging to its last remnant of colonial control. The political and moral standing of Irish republicanism had never been higher.

As the hunger strikers had died and as the H-Block/Armagh campaign had its impact, a process of republicanisation took place and at the end of all the most lasting effect of the campaign within the 6 counties was its educational value. Republicans who had done their time in prison and had subsequently dropped out of the movement — people with valuable experience and maturity — recognised that the hunger strikers were undergoing something far harder and harsher than anything they had had to suffer, and they came back to the movement. The hunger strike did away with spectator politics. When the only form of struggle being waged was armed struggle it only needed a small number of people to engage in it. But with the hunger strike people, rather than just looking on at one aspect of struggle, had an active role to play, which could be as limited or as important as billposting, writing letters, or taking part in numerous forms of protest.

The IRA eased back on operations during the hunger strike. But by the time a number of hunger strikers had died there was a considerable popular demand for the IRA to take punitive action. Toleration of the IRA increased very significantly, as did identification with it, and this had some strange consequences. There were occasions when IRA volunteers came out on the Falls to engage in armed action, only to have to withdraw because people were crowding around, applauding and patting them on the back.

Prior to the hunger strike we had been planning a slow build-up of electoral intervention, but we were impelled very rapidly into an instant, ill-prepared and insufficiently considered electoral strategy. The stunning initial success, with the election of Bobby Sands, the election of two prisoners in the 26 counties and the increased vote in Owen Carron's election, gave many of our members the impression that elections were all about winning. It was not until our second intervention in the 26 counties, when we tried to follow up the success of our prisoner candidates, that our members began to gain some kind of perspective.

The hunger strike and the electoral successes associated with it changed the course of the relationship between the republican movement and British strategy and set in train a process which continued through to the Hillsborough treaty. The perceived threat posed by republicanism since the hunger strike had led to the new, open relationship between Dublin and London, whereby the two governments are now *explicitly* engaged in collaboration on a joint policy, the overriding aim of which is to deal with the republican threat.

In 1976 the British government tried to criminalise the republican prisoners. In 1981 the republican prisoners criminalised the British government.

British Strategy

'For the British to calumniate Republicans and belittle their cause by besmirching them is one thing but for the Free State to do it is another, and different and worse thing. Because the British will not use British arguments to cloak their actions but Irish ones "out of our own mouths".'

Liam Mellows, 1922

'Ruling by fooling is a great British art — with great Irish fools to practise on.'

James Connolly, 1914

'The Prime Minister of Ireland . . . has accepted for all practical purposes and into perpetuity, that there will not be a united Ireland.'

Tom King, 1986

WOLFE TONE DESCRIBED the connection with England as 'the never failing source of all our political evils.' History has confirmed his view, for as long as Britain has sustained its intervention in Ireland it has prevented us from coming to grips with developing on our own terms, as people of all religious denominations and none, an Irish democracy.

The British government and army have no right to Ireland and no right to be in Ireland. Yet today they retain complete authority over the affairs of the people of the 6 counties and dominate the affairs of the people of the 26. They have never brought peace; rather, in pursuit of their own interests they have created and fostered bitter divisions.

Ireland is historically, culturally and geographically one single unit. The partition of Ireland, established by the British 'Government of Ireland Act' and subsequent British Acts, divides Ireland into two artificial statelets, the boundaries of which were determined by a sectarian head-count and can be maintained only by continuing sectarianism. As the English writer, C.P. Scott wrote of partition in 1920, it was done 'to entrench the 6 counties against Nationalist Ireland. Its effect will not be to make a solution of the Irish question easier but harder by creating a fresh and powerful obstacle.'

The British connection has lasted through several stages for many centuries and whether economic, political, territorial or cultural in substance it has used violence, coercion, sectarianism and terrorism as its principle methods of wielding power and exercising control. It has produced governments which have terrorised to maintain the status quo, organisations which fight to maintain their own privileged positions within it and organisations which fight in opposition to it. It has established partition, fear, distrust, sectarian privilege and poverty, disunity and faction fighting. It has brought death to many Irish people, to its own British soldiers and to English civilians.

The British connection denies civil and human rights to the Irish people and is maintained by concentration camps, summary executions, torture, paid perjurors and kangaroo courts. By its very nature the British presence is not and never has been a just or peaceful presence and because of this relationships between the Irish and British peoples have been poisoned. When the root cause of violence in Ireland is removed then and only then will the violence cease. Then the people of Ireland and Britain will find common cause to move forward into an era of mutual respect and solidarity which has been denied them by successive British governments.

The system established by Britain in the 6 counties created and constitutes the prop on which sectarianism depends. Its essential basis is the holding by a 'pro-British' national minority of a position of privilege over a dispossessed majority. It is important to recognise the often-ignored truth that this utterly undemocratic system was established, is controlled by and is the responsibility of the British government. The 'pro-British' elements will face up to the reality of the situation only when the British prop and the system which uses them as its tools and its stormtroopers is removed.

The British presence is not a matter only of the army and governmental institutions. It is also a matter of the domination of the economy. As James Connolly wrote,

> the subjection of one nation to another, as of Ireland to the
> authority of the British Crown, is a barrier to the free political
> and economic development of the subjected nation, and can
> only serve the interests of the exploiting classes of both nations.

Partition has divided the Irish economy into two parts which
were forced to lean separately on Britain. The 6 counties is a
dependent enclave within the UK economy, without any powers
of economic development or initiative of its own. It has no power
to control capital movements, to set up state industries of its own
or to vary the exchange rate so as to promote economic and
employment growth. The population of the 6 counties amounts
to only 2½ per cent of the population of the 'United Kingdom'.
It is a tiny minority in an area on the fringe of British economic
development.

Within an independent Ireland the political and economic
weight of the north's population would be greater in relation
to a national government than it is now in relation to the London parliament. While the British retain control the 6 counties
will suffer further de-industrialisation and greater dependency
on politically motivated hand-outs from Britain. Despite such
hand-outs there has been an enormous decline in employment,
at rates of between 55 and 85 per cent from 1952 to 1984 in
agriculture, ship building and textiles.

Foreign ownership of the north's manufacturing industry is
now about three-quarters of the total. Gross earnings have always
been lower and unemployment figures higher than in the rest
of the 'UK'. The Isles and Cuthbert report and others have identified the reasons for all this as being the narrow industrial structure in the 6 counties, a narrowness deriving from the role of
the 6 counties as a peripheral area within the 'UK' and also from
the fact of its separation from its natural hinterland, the 26 counties. This problem is most acutely seen in the special social and
economic problems affecting the border areas because of partition. These areas have been turned into peripheral areas within
the 6 and 26 county states, with their natural economic links
severed by decades of partition. In the 6 counties this problem
was increased by the discrimination by the Stormont regime
against towns like Strabane, Newry and Derry.

As a regional economy on the periphery of the 'UK' it suffers also from the wholesale export of capital. For example, according to the Hall Report it is estimated that the amount of 'Northern Ireland capital held outside Northern Ireland exceeded the amount of external capital held in Northern Ireland.' The consequences have been higher rates of poverty, unemployment, bad housing, demoralisation and ill-health.

The economy of the 26 counties has been similarly distorted by partition, which separated the larger part of the island from its northern industrial base and reduced the size of the home market. The neo-colonial character of the 26 counties was clear from the start; Lord Birkenhead, in defending the signing of the Treaty in the British House of Commons, described it as a matter of protecting British interests on the island with an economy of British lives. Thus they developed a neo-colonial relationship in which it was possible to protect their economic and strategic interests without the nuisance of having to occupy, garrison and administer the 26 counties.

The economy of the 26 counties is dominated by foreign capital; massive proportions of the profits generated in Irish industry are exported, in particular to Britain. The resources of the state are controlled and exploited by foreign interests and even the ruling class is not based principally on native capitalism but is an 'agent' class, acting as agents for foreign capital. This ruling class, put into power by the British, appreciates that its interests lie in the maintenance of partition and feels its interests threatened by popular political struggle; economic dependence on Britain translates in terms of political interest.

While the existence of a degree of political autonomy in the 26 counties, under the 1921 arrangement, enabled some economic progress to be made, this was at great social cost and on the basis of new kinds of neo-colonial dependence upon Britain. The loss of 29 per cent of the population and 40 per cent of the taxable capacity of the country, as well as the main industrial area and the largest city, Belfast — a port through which passed one third of the national trade before partition — meant that any attempt to build a viable economy would be doomed to failure. The loss of the industrial area around Belfast was particularly important. Metal goods had to be imported from Britain and paid for in goods Britain would accept. These were agricultural, mainly cattle. So dependent did the 26 counties become on this trade that in the 1950s the population was decreased to its lowest numbers while the state carried the highest number of cattle in its history. Indeed, since the Free State was established half of its population has had to emigrate.

A whole network of small farming communities was broken up and economically exiled as more and more land was gobbled up by big ranchers. The disparity in prices between the beef exports and the industrial imports affected the process of capital formation. It strengthened the power of mercantile as opposed to industrial interest and it encouraged capital to migrate. The deficiency arising from the adverse balance of trade — due to the failure of the cattle trade to earn enough to pay for industrial imports — increased the reliance on foreign capital as the principal motor of economic development. This accelerated from 1958 and led to the absorption of the 26 counties into the EEC on Britain's coat-tails.

Ireland is now a small, divided and powerless part of a new kind of collective imperialism in Europe, an economic arm of NATO and part of a common front of ex-colonial powers against the Third World. The new EEC treaty on European Union (the Single European Act), supported by Fine Gael and currently under consideration in Leinster House, will, if ratified there, commit the Dublin government to supporting a NATO view of international affairs and will abandon absolutely any remaining vestige of 'neutrality' or of Irish independence in foreign affairs. While EEC membership has seen the further erosion of Irish sovereignty and control of natural resources, the dependency of the 26 counties on Britain is seen in its foreign trade which is still 50 per cent with Britain. And despite the increase in American, German, French and Japanese investors, British investors still run the largest bloc of its manufacturing industry.

The small size of the domestic market and its excessively 'open' character is perhaps the most extreme in the developed world. This was caused directly by partition and worsened by the EEC. Before EEC membership, because of the dependency on foreign imports and the influence these had on shaping the capital formation, it would have been difficult for even a radical Dublin government to foster output and employment throughout the state. Now, EEC membership makes it 'illegal' to take the normal steps to control capital movement or to initiate state intervention by means of quotas, tariffs or aids to Irish industry.

Not only has partition and British domination of the economy distorted the economic potential of the country but it has also stunted the development of class politics. The trade union movement has been subjected to this general distortion. Any Dublin-based movement immediately evokes a hostile reaction from the loyalist workforce in the 6 counties and any London-based movement has a tendency to become at least benignly imperialistic. The Stormont government refused to deal with the Irish Congress of Trade Unions (ICTU) until it established a separate northern committee, thus ensuring loyalist domination of trade union affairs in the 6 counties and a major influence in British trade unions' attitudes to Ireland. The trade union movement failed to develop policies against discrimination and lost altogether the socialist republican legacy of James Connolly. The same problems that beset the trade union movement applied in the case of building a class-based socialist party.

Ordinary people throughout Ireland have absorbed the reality of their powerlessness under British domination, whether in colonial or neo-colonial form. The resources of the country lie far beyond their reach and all the decisive elements of the economy, even of society in general, are outside their control. When it comes to an industrial dispute very often the workers cannot even get to grips with their real opponents, the foreign owners and the central decision makers of the multinationals. The government and other political and religious elements step in and warn about job losses; they complain that if the workers continue with their action the foreign company that employs them will leave the country and that Ireland's image as a place for investment will be tarnished, with the result that other foreign companies will not invest and other jobs will not be created.

Multinationals are presented by the government with the people's money and the people's labour; then they take away the profit that is created by the people. Even within the terms of capitalism it is an absurd situation. Successive Dublin governments have claimed to base themselves upon the Proclamation of 1916, yet far from the ownership of Ireland belonging to the people of Ireland, it is clear that the economy is planned in the interests of a very small clique. The Proclamation talks about cherishing all the children of the nation equally, but the reality expressed in constant emigration is that the children of the nation not only could not be cherished equally; they were forced to leave and continue to be forced to leave.

Partition subverts the aim of an economy which can fulfill the domestic needs of the Irish people. The 26 counties has the highest youth population in western Europe and the highest aged population, and these people need a whole infrastructure of schools, houses, factories and roads; yet in all these respects the economy and the state are unable to deliver. We have an agricultural country which is given over to big ranching interests exporting beef; our horticultural imports undermine attempts to build up home-based industries.

A pre-condition for creating an economy which is able to deliver on the promise of the Proclamation, which is able even just to provide a living for its citizens in their own country, is independence. At present the 6 counties is administered directly in the British interest and the 26 counties is administered by Dublin governments whose economic planning is determined by British and other outside interests. The only way forward is to create an economy based on the needs of the Irish people.

In the 6 counties British control involves the maintenance of structural discrimination. For a long time discrimination in employment has been a feature of life, and furthermore those Catholics fortunate enough to get work suffer from discrimination in the type of job open to them. These are mostly in seasonal or unskilled occupations; in white collar and public sector jobs Catholics find their promotional opportunities severely restricted, rarely rising to executive or managerial level.

Some Unionists maintain, despite the evidence, that there was never any discrimination. Of those who reluctantly accept its existence, most maintain that it has now been eliminated. This is not the case. Since direct rule a more sophisticated approach in terms of presentation regarding discrimination has been adopted and in 1976 discrimination was declared illegal, yet no meaningful measures were undertaken to reverse the structural inequality. Legal platitudes or rhetoric cannot change reality, nor are they intended to; they are only meant to disguise it. Even the British government's own Department of Economic Development had to conclude in its 1986 report entitled *Equality of Op-*

portunity in Employment in Northern Ireland that 'the message of equality of opportunity in employment does not appear to be making a significant impact in relation to any dimension.'

One of the main features of discrimination lies in the actual structure of the economy which, broadly speaking, is based on those areas with a Protestant majority. Thus we have a disparity between the mainly Catholic rural west and the mainly Protestant industrial east; and even within these regions unemployment figures are much higher in areas with a Catholic majority as is demonstrated by the following Table:

Unemployment Rates by District Council Area, Sex and Religion (%)

District	Male		Female	
	Catholic	Protestant	Catholic	Protestant
Antrim	24.5	10.5	20.4	9.6
Ards	21.2	9.8	12.0	9.8
Armagh	28.8	10.2	15.9	9.5
Ballymena	22.1	11.1	14.0	9.0
Ballymoney	30.0	16.4	13.7	9.1
Banbridge	23.1	11.0	18.9	9.8
Belfast	31.4	15.6	18.3	14.1
Carrickfergus	20.5	22.7	8.9	10.6
Castlereagh	8.6	9.2	6.9	16.4
Coleraine	27.5	16.4	13.9	10.1
Cookstown	43.3	14.4	26.6	12.6
Craigavon	30.4	11.0	19.5	9.6
Down	19.7	8.9	11.6	9.0
Dungannon	36.7	12.7	24.0	11.6
Fermanagh	30.1	11.1	17.1	9.6
Larne	34.0	13.1	13.7	10.9
Limavady	36.7	14.3	16.2	11.4
Lisburn	22.1	8.8	15.8	9.6
Derry	35.8	14.4	17.6	10.1
Magherafelt	31.9	16.5	17.5	11.0
Moyle	31.1	21.0	16.2	15.1
Newry & Mourne	35.5	14.8	20.0	12.0
Newtownabbey	18.1	11.8	11.5	8.9
North Down	11.1	7.1	9.2	7.0
Omagh	27.2	10.9	15.6	9.4
Strabane	39.0	21.9	20.4	13.6

Source: 1981 Population Census, unpublished data.

Note: The true figures for Catholic unemployment rates may actually be higher; the 1981 census was boycotted by many nationalists in protest at the British government's 'criminalisation' policy.

The 23 per cent overall unemployment figures in the 6 counties disguise considerable regional imbalances between, for example, Castlereagh at 8.6 per cent male Catholic unemployment and Ballymurphy at 82 per cent. Even these figures are in reality much higher because since November 1982 unemployment figures have been artificially lowered by excluding unemployed people not claiming benefit and those temporarily on unemployed training schemes.

The facts of discrimination under the old Stormont regime are well documented elsewhere. The facts of discrimination under direct British rule are revealed with great regularity by the British government's own Fair Employment Agency, and there is no evidence of any real change. For example, less than five per cent of the workforce in Short's is Catholic and this despite assurances from British Ministers that there would be equality in employment and equality in opportunity of employment. The very few large-scale British government-sponsored investment incentives have been aimed directly at undermining support for republicanism — a foolish and spurious reason for investment, as witness the De Lorean fiasco. None have made any impact on redressing the balance of employment on a regional basis. During the economic boom the opportunity to do this was not taken and in the post-oil crisis situation of recession the introduction of Thatcherite monetarist policies has made matters worse.

Structural inequalities have been reiterated and reinforced since the introduction of direct rule while the overall situation of the peripheral economy has declined, with more closures and massive redundancies. The policy of cut-backs has meant an increase in unemployment across the board, with structural discrimination remaining as much a feature as ever.

* * *

Britain's economic interests in Ireland and their consequences represent, however, only one thread on the loom of colonial control and intervention. The strategic reasons behind the initial English conquest remain to some extent centuries later, and I do not believe that the British government has at any time in the last twenty years seriously considered leaving Ireland. Not because Ireland has failed to feature as a priority but because they accept the situation as it is. Many commentators suggest that a problem with the British government is that they are always concerned with other priorities. I do not believe that that is a real problem; the fact of the matter is that they just accept that the 6 counties are part of their set-up, their 'United Kingdom'.

In spite of the technology of modern warfare Ireland represents a strategic area of some importance. Economically, Ireland is at the very least a considerable marketplace and its industrial base is dominated from Britain. Politically, it has been argued that for Britain to unwind its relationship with Ireland would be to unwind the whole nature of the British state. Any radicalisation of Irish society becomes a threat to the British establishment to the extent that it offers encouragement to people in Britain and has a radicalising effect in specifically British political terms.

It is not, however, out of the question that in certain circumstances the British government would find a United Ireland completely acceptable. Their attitude has consistently been towards all of Ireland. Even the basis on which the 6 and 26 county states were established provided for a Council of Ireland, and one can argue that partition was seen only as a temporary necessity to consolidate in a territorial sense British control over part of Ireland as the bridgehead of its influence over the whole island. Territorial unity of the 6 and 26 counties would not necessarily threaten British interests; indeed, the Dublin government now acts as a junior partner in relation to London, expressing the thread of common interest that has always existed between the Irish and British ruling classes.

What threatens British government interests is not the simple joining together of two partitioned statelets into their one geographical unit. The prospect that threatens them is national self-determination: a united nation defining and implementing independent policies both internally and externally, acting in the interests of the Irish people as a whole. Such an independent Ireland would pass out of Britain's combined colonial and neo-colonial control.

The right-wing Tory Monday Club has warned of the danger of Ireland becoming a Cuba on Britain's doorstep. I do not believe that there is any real basis for that scenario but it is nevertheless understandable that NATO and the Western Alliance are implacably opposed to an independent Ireland which would not be aligned with them. Under the present arrangement, because of Britain's membership of NATO, this military alliance has a foothold in Ireland with the 6 counties incorporated directly into NATO.

National self-determination would mean the Irish people defining their foreign policy in their own interests and fraternally in the interests of those with whom we could identify in a general sense. It would mean alignment with emerging small nations, with ex-colonies, with people struggling for self-determination and equality, and against the big power blocs.

Irish foreign policy would be based on positive neutrality, not the mediocre notion which is sometimes pontificated upon by Dublin politicians but an active, positive policy of neutrality opposed to militarisation, the arms race, the threat of nuclear annihiliation and working for the internationalism of, as Connolly put it, 'a free federation of free peoples'. An independent Ireland would develop relationships with other countries to their mutual advantage and to the general benefit of humankind. The suggestion that Irish neutrality should be swapped for Irish unity and independence is a contradiction in terms, for neutrality and independence must be two sides of the one coin.

In its foreign policy an independent Ireland could play a positive role as a catalyst, but we should not have an inflated sense of our own importance. Some people have the rather chauvinist idea that Ireland would take its place at the head of small nations; such a notion is unrealistic, but in various small ways there is no doubt that Ireland could intervene against the domination of the power blocs which constantly threatens the world with nuclear catastrophe. To take one appropriately small example, the Band Aid appeal obviously caught the imagination of young people in Ireland. What an Irish government should have been doing at the same time was using its influence to demand change of those countries that monopolise and destroy food products on a regular basis. An independent Irish foreign policy would seek to intervene to subvert the stranglehold of a world economic order which squeezes large parts of Africa dry and promotes the most reactionary and oppressive regimes worldwide.

The strategic concerns of British policy towards Ireland have obviously undergone many changes of emphasis over the centuries. In recent decades its strategic interest has been one shared, by and large, by the western European and US governments: for the maintenance of stability and social order in capitalist Europe. Britain, in the post-colonial era, does not act alone in the grand manner of its imperial heyday. Indeed, it is reduced on occasions to acting simply as the US government's largest aircraft carrier. But the traditional British claim to the territory of Ireland is buttressed by the US and western European concern to maintain the status quo, and in pursuit of this kind of 'stability' the British government has employed a wide variety of techniques of oppression.

Between 1800 and 1921 the British government enacted 105 separate coercion acts dealing with Ireland. *Habeas corpus* was frequently suspended and the jails of Ireland and the penal colonies in Australia were regularly populated by Irish political prisoners. Since partition this policy of coercion, modernised and updated, has continued.

From the establishment of the Northern Ireland state Britain has armed and financed a sectarian apparatus of repression. By 1922 it had organised, armed and was paying for a combined force of over 45,000 loyalists in the 6 counties, made up of 'A', 'B' and 'C' Specials whose memberships were based upon the loyalist paramilitary organisation, the Ulster Volunteer Force (UVF), and the RUC. These so-called 'security forces' were employed in an openly partisan political manner to suppress nationalist opposition and were backed up by an array of repressive laws. Internment was provided for and was used to suppress anti-Unionists. Judges were almost all openly associated with the ruling Unionist Party.

Britain began by 'arming the Protestants', to use the phrase that provides the title for Michael Farrell's study of the formation of the Specials and the RUC, and by establishing the 'Protestant parliament for a Protestant people' together with an administration and judiciary which were overwhelmingly loyalist. Having achieved this, their strategy consisted simply of supporting the Stormont government as the basis of social and political stability.

From 1969, however, Britain has exercised a greater degree of direct control, replacing the 'B' Specials with the Ulster

Defence Regiment (UDR), which, while almost identical in composition to the 'B' Specials, was and is under the control of the British army, and initially placing British army regiments in the front line of confrontation with the nationalists, in response to the RUC's failure to hold that line. In the period immediately after 1969 the British government made noises about introducing liberal reforms but made no move towards implementation of such reforms as would have given the 6 counties the elements of 'British democracy' such as the separation of powers and the impartial administration of justice. Instead the nature of the change in British strategy at this time was simply that it took over direct responsibility for the exercise of coercion.

The powers of suppression which had been exercised through the RUC and Specials were now taken over for intensified use by the British army. The strategy of military coercion took the forms of large-scale information-gathering exercises, detention for questioning, internment and detention without trial. On the day in August 1971 when internment was introduced 342 people were arrested; within six months 2,357 were arrested, of whom 1,600 were released. A number of those who were interned were subjected to torture using sensory deprivation techniques. From 1972 detention without trial replaced internment.

The introduction of the Northern Ireland (Emergency Provisions) Act in August 1973 extended RUC and British army powers and set aside standard provisions of the law; it included the abolition of juries, fundamental changes in the rules of evidence, and extensive powers to detain for questioning. This provided the legal framework for the British army to conduct intensive intelligence screening, in-depth interrogation, house searches and frequent arrests for questioning including large-scale arrest operations. In 1971 there were 17,262 house searches; in 1973 the number rose to 75,000, one fifth of the number of houses in the whole of the 6 counties; almost every house searched was in a nationalist area. Further repressive powers were brought in with the Prevention of Terrorism Act in 1974, yet even this vast armoury of powers was exceeded by many British army operations which were clearly illegal.

Other British army tactics included the use of agents provocateurs, assassination squads, 'counter-gangs', undercover units, the computerisation of intelligence information and new crowd control and surveillance techniques. The 6 counties became a laboratory of techniques and tactics of political suppression and counter-insurgency, all of which were directed exclusively against the nationalist population. British strategy up to the end of 1975 was, in summary, to conduct a war of political suppression, with the British army playing the leading role.

By 1975 the British government had begun to implement its strategy of 'Ulsterisation' and 'criminalisation', which in broad terms sought to deny the political nature of the struggle while at the same time refining and renewing the forms of suppression. The RUC were brought back again to a position from which it was intended that they should step into the front line. They were made into more of an army than a police force; their intelligence capabilities were built up, with special emphasis on the use of informers, surveillance and detention for questioning. This strategy, which aimed for 'normalisation', had been a major strand of British strategy since 1972, one which they had hoped to have fully operational by 1975. The British government have also used bilateral truces with the IRA to gain the upper hand, to cause confusion in republican ranks and to introduce new strategies. They have never engaged in a truce with the serious intention of considering or conceding the republican demands. In particular, the lengthy bilateral truce of 1974-75 was used to push ahead with the Ulsterisation/normalisation/criminalisation policy. However, the resumption of military struggle by the IRA prevented the successful implementation of their timetable.

Placing renewed emphasis on the courts, rather than internment, as a means of disposing of their nationalist opponents, the British government opened both Castlereagh and Gough Barracks interrogation centres in 1977. These were designed to supply, through the systematic application of torture techniques, the statements required to secure convictions in the courts. As early as April 1977 the Association of Forensic Medical Officers made representations to the Police Authority, and in November Amnesty International conducted an investigation. 86 per cent of all defendants appearing before Diplock Courts between January and April 1979 had made confessions; 56 per cent of prosecutions in relation to these relied solely on confessions, while another 30 per cent relied primarily on confessions.

'Criminalisation' aimed at isolating the republican resistance. Another form of isolation aimed at was geographical: the development of 'counter-insurgency architecture' whereby the RUC and British army were closely involved in local authority planning in the interests of counter-insurgency and the control of urban populations, with particular emphasis on confining nationalists within ghettoes with a limited number of access and exit points. Powers of arrest and detention were used even more than before as a control and intimidation technique and for intelligence gathering and screening. In the ten months between 1 January and 30 October 1980, 3,868 people were arrested under the Emergency Provisions Act and the Prevention of Terrorism Act and detained for more than four hours; of these only 11 per cent were charged. The primacy of the RUC was further developed by the creation of special units which received training from the British army's SAS in the techniques that equipped them to carry out a British government-approved 'shoot-to-kill' policy against republicans.

In 1977 Roy Mason, Britain's Northern Ireland Secretary, genuinely thought he had the situation under control, that the project of pacifying the 6 counties was on the verge of completion, and that the IRA were being 'squeezed like toothpaste'. It was an appreciation of the falseness of Mason's view which led to the production of Brigadier Glover's report in late 1978 and the recognition that the element of British strategy which required the military suppression of the resistance could not be implemented. Nevertheless, the 'criminalisation' policy continued to be pursued energetically and such were the contradictions of the overall strategy that it succeeded in generating both unprecedented support for the IRA and a new political obstacle in the form of Sinn Féin's dramatic electoral successes.

The cutting edge of the British strategy of 'criminalisation' was the attempt to abolish political prisoner status. But it was at this vital point that British strategy broke down. It had been delayed and frustrated in previous years by the republican resistance, but with the hunger strike, the mass campaign in support of the prisoners' demands and the Sinn Féin electoral achievements it suffered a substantial reverse.

At a time when, as far as the British were concerned, the IRA had been beaten into the ground and isolated; at a time, too, when British government funds were being pumped into the De Lorean car plant on the edge of West Belfast and into Leisure and Community Centres; at a time when the internees had been released and only a small number of 'criminals' remained in the H-Blocks, British strategy received a stunning blow. The mass campaign in support of the H-Block and Armagh prisoners, the heroic self-sacrifice of the hunger strikers, and the massive votes for Sinn Féin alerted the Dublin government, via the urgings of the SDLP, that they had surrendered the high ground of nationalism and that the only people articulating the nationalist position were the 'terrorists'. Dublin saw an urgent need, which it communicated to the British government, to build an alterntive to the 'terrorists' and to establish a context of credibility for establishment politics in order to undermine the substantial support that had been demonstrated for the republicans.

Since the first hunger strike, in December 1980, when a 'totality of relationships' was announced, through silver tea-pot diplomacy, a short-lived 'constitutional crusade', and the changes in governments which were as short on leadership as they were on days in office, Dublin and their northern allies, the SDLP, had been struggling to climb back to the heights of Irish nationalism which they had surrendered to the republicans. The Dublin Forum was the still-born child of that attempt and it was launched on 2 May 1984 after eleven months of deliberations and amidst unprecedented media hype.

Two months later John Hume of the SDLP delivered a presentation of the report at a much heralded debate on this document in the British House of Commons. Only 50 out of almost 700 British members of parliament turned up to hear him. Worse was to follow. On 19 November of that year Margaret Thatcher in her infamous 'Out, out, out' remarks, rejected the conclusions of the Forum report, humiliated the Irish establishment and stated clearly what issues would be on the agenda. Dublin's need to engage in nationalist rhetoric was of no importance to her. Charles Haughey's claims about a totality of relationships during previous talks would not be permitted to be repeated; new talks would clearly and unambiguously be about defeating 'terrorism'.

The British establishment — and in particular Sir Robert Armstrong, secretary to the British cabinet — had been influenced by a report entitled *Britain's Undefended Frontier: A Policy for Ulster*. This report, like the Dublin Forum report, was influenced by recent developments in the 6 counties. It was produced by a right-wing group within the British establishment, the Independent Study Group, and was launched in October 1984, published by the Institute for European Defence and Strategic Studies.

It recognised the problem of what is called 'nationalist alienation' from British institutions in the 6 counties and the dangers of this to Dublin. It promoted cross-border collaboration as the only alternative to a dangerous escalation of British repression which could provoke a nationalist backlash throughout Ireland. Among its proposals were included:

* a joint London-Dublin security commission, including a military sub-committee made up of representatives of both armed forces.

* a full-time secretariat drawn from Dublin and Whitehall civil servants.

* London-Dublin summits at fixed intervals.

In its text the report spoke of co-operation from northern nationalists only being won if 'they are bought by political concessions'. It outlined its view that Dublin had a crucial role to play in defeating the IRA, as had happened in the 1956-62 campaign which

> was a signal failure because London and Dublin were united in wholeheartedly opposing it and in particular because internment was in operation on both sides of the border. . . We think it should be made clear to the Dublin government that the degree of force which must be used [by the British] in the attempt to restore order will be in inverse proportion to the degree of effective co-operation on security which can be achieved between the two governments.

The report also advised,

> We believe that British policy has suffered in the past from an excessive and misconceived regard for the sensibilities of the Irish Republic [i.e. the Dublin government].

Margaret Thatcher's 'Out, out, out' rejection of the sensibilities of the Dublin government, delivered one month after this report was completed, showed that she had taken this point, at least, on board.

In addition to the impact of the hunger strikes and Sinn Féin electoral successes, the British government was also rudely awakened from complacency by the Brighton bombing. The full effects of this IRA operation will not become apparent until some British Minister writes his or her memoirs. But the fact is that Óglaigh na hÉireann almost wiped out the British cabinet and that fact awakened the government to the urgent need from their point of view to address themselves to the issues of Ireland and the IRA.

The stage was set for the Hillsborough talks and under the triple impacts of the hunger strike, the Sinn Féin vote and the Brighton bombing the Hillsborough treaty was forged. Prior to 1968 the British government had basically ignored the problems of structural discrimination and sectarian power in the 6 counties; it had been happy enough to leave the Unionists to get on with the business of running the place. With the failure of the Unionists to keep a lid on the situation, however, Britain became involved in direct intervention, took control of state functions and began to employ its own strategies in pursuit of stability under the Crown. What the Hillsborough treaty represents is a coming-together of the various British strategies on an all-Ireland basis, with the Dublin government acting as the new guarantor of partition.

In the final analysis the agreement is about stabilising British interests. It is about what the British and Dublin governments quaintly call 'security'. It addresses itself to a problem for the British outlined in Brigadier Glover's 1978 report: British army intelligence could do nothing about the structures and organisation of the IRA in the 26 counties; only 'security' harmonisation with Dublin could remedy this lack. It is also, of course, about the political context of what they call the 'security problem'. It is an attempt to isolate and draw popular support away from the republican struggle while putting a diplomatic veneer on British rule, injecting a credibility into establishment 'nationalism' so that British rule and the interests it represents can be stabilised in the long term, and insulating the British from international criticism of their involvement in Irish affairs.

The duration of the republican struggle and the failure of the

Unionists to defeat it were major factors in the British desire to modernise her colonial arrangements. They could afford to offend the Unionists; after all, there were to be no constitutional changes and the Unionists, for all their protestations, had failed to subdue opposition to partition. Their blatant use of discrimination, gerrymandering and coercion, encouraged by the British government for as long as they succeeded in fulfilling the British need to neutralise opposition to their rule in Ireland, now needed to be refined. And, as Sinn Féin warned before the Hillsborough treaty was signed, the predictable Unionist reaction was needed and would be utilised to exaggerate whatever concessions might be produced by the Hillsborough process.

The major achievement for the British government is that it has succeeded in publicly tying in the Dublin government as junior partner in its strategy. Dublin has thus become the guarantor of partition and the jewel in the crown of British strategy.

The SDLP, Loyalists and Republicans

Hapless Nation! Hapless Land!
Heap of uncementing sand!
Crumbled by a foreign weight:
and by worse, domestic hate.

William Drennan

SET UP IN August 1970 the SDLP consisted initially of six Stormont opposition MPs of diverse political backgrounds and attitudes. Three had been elected as independents; Gerry Fitt was the Republican Labour Party; Paddy Devlin was a member of the Northern Ireland Labour Party (NILP); and Austin Currie was a member of the Nationalist Party. In October 1970 the New Democratic Party, a reformist split from the Nationalist Party, dissolved into the SDLP. The new party also had strong links with elements in the 26 counties, particularly in Fianna Fáil, and it had links with the leadership of the British Labour Party, which may have played a significant role in advising its formation.

The Nationalist Party had until then monopolised anti-Unionist politics, but as well as superceding the old party the SDLP posed a middle-class alternative to the small republican and socialist groups which were emerging at the time in response to the crisis. Representing, especially in the person of John Hume, the middle-class response, the SDLP believed in establishing social democracy within the 6 county state. John Hume only became involved in the Derry civil rights situation after his refusal to sponsor the demonstration of 5 October 1968, and only when it became clear that the march had opened up a new dimension. In becoming involved he represented the reflex action of the middle class in seeking to ensure that a 'responsible' leadership took over from the assorted radicals and republicans who had been making the running.

Throughout their early history the SDLP shuffled from one position to another, responding to the public mood; they looked to see where the people were going so that they could lead them — a definition, in effect, of political opportunism. At the high tide of popular opposition to the state in 1971 their policy was one of opposition to the state. When, however, Prime Minister Brian Faulkner saw the need for a degree of Catholic middle class support for his policies, the SDLP responded immediately. On the one hand Faulkner announced that the British army would shoot anyone behaving suspiciously, while on the other hand committees were to be established, two of which would be chaired by members of the opposition, to examine and advise on policy regarding environmental and industrial services. The committees, while offering perks to members, were devoid of meaningful content, yet Paddy Devlin declared that they represented Faulkner's finest hour and John Hume announced that they provided an answer to all those people who had been saying that no change had taken place in the 6 counties.

On 7 July 1971 the SDLP were attending an all-party discussion under Faulkner's scheme; on the evening of the same day Seamus Cusack was shot dead by British soldiers in Derry, and on the following day Desmond Beattie was shot dead, also in Derry. While the SDLP were involved in one aspect of Faulkner's strategy nationalists were the victims of the other aspect of that strategy. Within a few days the SDLP were forced by popular sentiment to withdraw from the all-party discussions rather than to continue to give credibility to Faulkner's policies and to the state.

In October 1971 the Northern Resistance Movement (NRM) was formed, bringing together republicans, Peoples Democracy and progressive nationalists, and the People's Assembly of the New Lodge Road was established. The response of the SDLP was to set up an 'alternative assembly' at Dungiven, which was representative of the SDLP, the old Nationalist Party and certain local councillors, MPs and senators. It was shortlived but it was a symbolical exercise complete with all the trappings of parliamentarianism which sought merely to state some kind of establishment alternative to the NRM and the other manifestations of popular struggle. In succeeding years it has sought constantly to pose an alternative to whatever forms of struggle have developed on a popular level.

In 1973/74 the Sunningdale agreement and the power-sharing Executive had the effect of clarifying the role of the SDLP. It had left Stormont after the shooting of Cusack and Beattie; it had lent its name to the Rent and Rates Strike and the civil disobedience campaign in protest against internment; and it had pledged that it would not engage in talks while internment lasted. Yet, with internment still in existence it became involved in lengthy discussions with the very people it had pledged not to talk to, and in short-lived government in the Executive it showed itself as capable as the Unionists of dealing with protest by draconian measures.

During the Rent and Rates Strike well-known members of the SDLP told people not to bother to put by the money they were witholding in rents. Wiser counsels suggested banking it, putting it in the post office, forming a central fund or putting it into one account, but the SDLP just said, 'Don't worry about it'. Yet once in power in the Executive they introduced through Austin Currie a weekly levy for unpaid rents. This levy, which began the forced gathering of debts, provided the basis for some of the most exploitative legislation to be visited on the people of the 6 counties.

Even now there are old people whose electricity meters are 'governed', which means that, as a means of recovering debts, they get only 30p of electricity for every 50p they put in; similar devices are used in relation to gas. People are intimidated into signing 'voluntary' agreements covering payments and repayments. People who have had damages awarded to them for assault by the Crown forces and people who have received compensation for industrial accidents find that these amounts are actually set against debts that they have, so they may end up getting nothing. In one case livestock has been seized by the state, in a manner reminiscent of the Land War. Many people on social security do not actually receive money because their rent is taken out at source, as are their electricity and gas bills and any debt which relates to the public services. People are thus deprived of the elementary dignity of having the decision as to how and when they pay their bills and low-income families, whose plight is already made worse by public spending cuts, are thus placed under intolerable financial pressure. There have been suicides in the Divis Flats complex where a major contributory factor has been the Payment of Debts Act, and short of that people are driven to dependence on valium and the like.

The about-face on the Rent and Rates issue, with all its appalling consequences, illustrates well the nature and role of the SDLP. It shows the way in which the 'respectable' and 'responsible' politicians operate. The SDLP's participation in talks, in the Assembly and in the Executive was viewed with disgust not just by republicans but by ordinary Catholics, and this disgust was intensified, particularly in the working class, by their betrayal of the Rent and Rates Strike. From the point of view of British strategy the Sunningdale experience had succeeded for the first time in producing a fully-fledged Catholic partitionist party in the form of the SDLP, a party that was prepared to work the partitionist system.

The SDLP shares a perspective with the British government and often shows itself to be quite conscious of the fact. During the hunger strike it was only when Bobby Sands had died that they raised their voices to the British government and the concern they expressed was that Margaret Thatcher's stance was endangering Britain's overall strategic interest. Certainly the SDLP's role in British strategy was weakened by its isolation during the hunger strike. As the massive funeral for Patsy O'Hara in Derry passed John Hume's house someone was at the window looking out and the curtain was dropped as the head of the procession passed. It may not, of course, have been John Hume at the window but nevertheless it provided a symbol of the temporary isolation of the SDLP.

In response to the upheaval and mass mobilisation of the H-Block/Armagh campaign, with its intensified support for militant republicanism, the SDLP sought a means to make so-called constitutional nationalism relevant, and so they elaborated the plan for the Dublin Forum, adapting ideas first developed by the Irish Independence Party in relation to a Council of Ireland. The crisis posed for them and for the Dublin government was a very sharp one, involving as it did a hung parliament at Leinster House. It is no coincidence that it was in the wake of the hunger strike that one saw the emergence of a clear community of interest between the 26 county political establishment, the Catholic church hierarchy and the SDLP. They were united not simply against what they term 'the men of violence' — the IRA — but against a popular struggle of resistance to British rule in the 6 counties which materially threatened their shared self-interest. They had been rudely awakened by the hunger strike campaign to the fact that there was a pressing need to rebuild the credibility of the SDLP.

The appreciation of this need was not restricted to Irish or British government interests. In June 1985 it was announced in New York that the National Democratic Institute for International Affairs (NDIIA) was to help the SDLP. The NDIIA and its Republican counterpart operate on grants from the National Endowment for Democracy, established by the US Congress in 1983 in response to a call from Ronald Reagan for 'a global capacity to foster the infrastructure of democracy'. The Endowment for Democracy has interfered in elections in Central and South America, has sponsored dubious political projects in the Philippines, India and South Africa, and has given support to right-wing student and trade union bodies in France. SDLP leader John Hume has welcomed and defended his party's receiving assistance from the NDIIA.

The SDLP has always figured prominently in the Dublin and Westminster governments' strategies and both governments have in different periods sought to buttress the position of the SDLP as the politically professional and respectable representatives of the nationalist population. Its importance in British strategy lies in the fact that the days of the one-party state in the 6 counties are over: the sins of the Stormont administration are internationally known and public opinion would not accept a return to the status quo of the 'Protestant parliament for a Protestant people'. The establishment by the British of devolved government involving the participation of the SDLP could be presented as being representative of what they would call 'all sections of the community'. The role of the SDLP is that of a kind of 'Uncle Tom' element that the British government needs in order to stabilise the situation, and its leadership has played its role consistently and well.

The support of the SDLP leadership for the Hillsborough treaty, a treaty which could not have been signed by the Dublin government without SDLP approval, is a current example of how important a role the SDLP plays in the on-going strategy to undermine the legitimate Irish demand for national self-determination and sovereignty. The SDLP's efforts to stabilise the 6 county situation run parallel to British aims and have been consistently pitched within the parameters laid down by the British government.

Since the Hillsborough treaty the SDLP has increasingly found itself cast in the role of Fine Gael's northern representatives and, as the high falutin' promises it made about substantial concessions flowing from the Hillsborough treaty have failed to materialise, SDLP spokespersons find themselves also in the embarrassing position of acting as apologists for the British government, while at the same time criticising that government.

John Hume has never made any secret of his political philosophy, of his admiration for European-style social democratic politics and of his rejection of nationalism as an outdated concept. Seamus Mallon, the deputy leader, has, however, projected himself for years as the nationalist conscience of the SDLP. He was outspoken in his criticism of the Dublin Forum options — calling them 'a bag of dolly mixtures' — and yet he dramatically changed course and accepted these options, perhaps more for personal reasons than for any clear political reason.

Mr Mallon's abandonment of Irish nationalism at this time, though he still uses nationalist rhetoric and is in many ways a likeable model of the old-style Irish nationalist politician, removed from the SDLP leadership any remaining vestige of nationalist or separatist sentiment. No Irish nationalist could support any treaty which institutionalises British government claims to a part of Irish national territory. Indeed the term — 'constitutional nationalism' — used by Mr Mallon and his colleagues to describe their political philosophy is a contradiction in terms. The only constitutional nationalist in Irleand today is Sean McBride. He puts his nationalism within a framework of Irish constitutionality. Mr Mallon, however, puts his within the framework of British constitutionality. Irish nationalism within British constitutionality is a contradiction in terms.

Members of the SDLP leadership are outspoken in their opposition to Sinn Féin and in their hostility to the IRA, and that, of course, is their right, but their extreme language about 'evildoers, men of violence and paramilitary terrorists' is never used in relation to British forces or their political masters. They reserve their vitriolic abuse for republicans and have also on occasions committed the very sins of exclusion which they used so often to accuse the Unionists of. For example, the SDLP was party to Sinn Féin's exclusion from the Dublin Forum, despite our clear electoral support, and the SDLP has refused on a number of occasions to talk to the Sinn Féin leadership, a result, obviously, of its support for Unionist, London and Dublin attempts to ostracise us politically.

One consistent strand in SDLP strategy has been its willingness to accommodate the loyalists and to accuse the republicans of being sectarian.

Republicanism is nothing if it is not resolutely anti-sectarian. That statement may be received with scorn by those who seek to equate republicanism with a certain tradition of Catholic nationalism. But Irish republicanism is, almost by definition, an ideology of the dispossessed seeking equality. Of course, if you seek rights of which you have been deprived, those who have deprived you of those rights and those who have appropriated those rights to themselves will appreciate that your equality can only be achieved by depriving them of their position of privilege. If the black people of South Africa achieve equality with other races, they cannot do so other than at the expense of those who have deprived them of equality and monopolised social and economic privilege — namely the whites. Is it therefore racist of the blacks to seek equality? Of course not.

Unionism and loyalism require a Protestant ascendancy — that is their raison d'être. Their political philosophy expresses loyalty to the union with Britain precisely and solely because that union has to date guaranteed them their privileges and their ascendancy. At the level of the Unionist ruling class that privilege may be substantial and real. At the level of the working class it may be more perceived than real and to the extent that it is real it may be marginal, but it is often marginal privilege which is most fiercely fought for.

Unionism requires a one-party state and requires the suppression of significant opposition. It has not only failed to become engaged even within the confines of the state in power-sharing, it has also failed absolutely to come to terms with the simple human proposition that the man or woman down the road has an equal right to vote, an equal right to job opportunities, and an equal right to housing.

The resolute anti-sectarianism of republicanism is not new and it is not confined to what may be termed the radical element of the tradition. This correct attitude sometimes leads republicans into ignoring loyalism as a political threat altogether and misunderstanding can arise about the exact nature of loyalism.

Colonial powers have long used the plantation of garrisons to keep down rebellious natives. These garrisons were given privileges in return for their loyalty, and these privileges usually included the lands and property of the dispossessed natives. So it was in Ireland. The garrisons were also usually in some way different from the natives. In other colonies there was a racial and often a colour difference. In Ireland the division was religious and sectarianism was the prop or privilege by which this division was maintained.

So it is that every push against the British by the republicans and every gain won by nationalists is seen inevitably as a threat to the Unionist position. The demand for 'One man, one vote' was seen by Unionists as a threat. And it was a threat: a threat to Unionist privilege. Once that demand was won the Unionists lost control of Derry, 'their' Maiden City.

No matter what demands one makes of the state, even trying to get a grant for a Gaelic football pitch or seeking to put up a street sign in the Irish language, these demands are seen by Unionists as posing threats. No matter how non-sectarian one's intentions, the reaction by the Unionist politicians is that one is encroaching on their area of privilege, that one is, in fact, threatening 'the Protestant way of life'.

This was not always the case. In the 1790s Belfast was the centre of an Irish political movement which linked Antrim and Down with the Republics of France and America, and Belfast citizens celebrated the Fall of the Bastille, drank toasts of Mirabeau and Lafayette and studied Paine's great book, *The Rights of Man*. Presbyterians formed the Society of United Irishmen and declared for Catholic emancipation, for the abolition of church establishments and of tithes, for resistance to rack-rents and for sweeping agrarian reforms. They gave a cordial welcome to Mary Wollstonecraft's *Vindication of the Rights of Women* and joined with their Catholic neighbours in the struggle for natural independence and political democracy.

Yet within two generations the majority of Presbyterians had completely abandoned their revolutionary principles, embraced the politics of the Tories and developed a deep-rooted antipathy towards their Catholic neighbours. This transformation, as the historian Andrew Boyd correctly states, is one of the most disturbing facts of Irish history. It was caused directly by the forces of reaction, supported by the wealthy landlord class who feared the union of Protestant, Catholic and Dissenter.

The Presbyterians, then as now, were the largest religious denomination apart from the Catholics. Had they remained untouched by the neo-fascism of Orangeism they would, in alliance with their Catholic countrymen, have undoubtedly transformed Irish society. They were, however, deeply divided, one faction headed by Thomas Cooke, a narrow-minded Paisley-type Tory, the other led by Henry Montgomery, a liberal whose father had been an officer in the battle of Antrim in 1798. Montgomery made no secret of his liberal political and religious principles. He campaigned for Catholic emancipation, was proud of his republican background and forthright in theological and political disputes with Cooke. Cooke, who was equally forthright in his views, was deeply anti-Catholic, and one of his ancestors had fought on the Williamite side during the wars at the end of the seventeenth century. He hated the United Irishmen and their democratic separatist principles and campaigned for control of Ireland's Presbyterians. He found support among the Tories, the landowning class and the Orange lodges and eventually succeeded in ousting Montgomery who left the parent church and formed the non-subscribing Presbyterian Church.

Cooke, secure in leadership of the Presbyterian Church, built up a powerful politico-religious movement in which the Orange order, by then nearly forty years in existence, was to play a major part. The Orange order, an exclusively Protestant and bitterly anti-Catholic organisation, had been formed in 1795 to protect poorer Protestant farmers and rich Protestant landlords; it was an alliance of the landed gentry and those poorer Protestants who were united in their distrust of liberalism and Irish Catholics. Until Cooke's time the Orange order had made little impact on the Presbyterians, and the first Orangemen were decendants of the English rather than the Scottish planters. Under Cooke this situation changed dramatically and the Presbyterians were drawn increasingly away from radicalism to Toryism and the political cult of Orangeism. Political and religious bigotry of the most extreme description were fused together and, as the power of Orangeism increased Belfast saw the first of the riots with which we are so familiar to the present day.

Loyalism, with its bigoted and irrational hatred of Catholics and its conservative politics, has nothing to do with the Protestant religion. Due to historical circumstances the Protestant religion has been continually dragged into association with it and religion, in particular Protestantism, has been brought into disrepute by this association.

Loyalism as such is not based on religious considerations. Rather, it is based on power, a power which is perceived as being unsustainable without the subservience of the Catholic population. From the smooth tones of upper-class 'respectable' Unionists to the virulent hate-mongering of loyalist paramilitaries the same impression emerges of Catholics as a sub-species. But the hatred and contempt relate clearly to the question of power, and the responsibility for this rests with the British government.

It was a political crisis in Britain which led to the playing of the Orange card in Ireland and to the rekindling of sectarianism and the birth of modern loyalism. This occurred when the British Liberal Party commenced the democratisation of the political system in Britain by measures aimed at reducing the authority of the House of Lords over the Commons, thus curtailing the power of the British landlords and aristocrats.

The Liberals were at this time the voice of British democracy. They represented the sensible capitalist classes who had emerged during the industrial revolution. They had no time for aristocratic superstitions, the Divine Right of Kings or the House of Lords. The Tories, on the other hand, were interested only in preserving their political power in the British parliamentary system. They had a 'born to rule' mentality and were outraged at the erosion of their power which occurred in the latter half of the 19th century as the Liberals extended voting rights to the ordinary British people.

At the same time the Home Rule movement, led by Parnell and aimed at breaking the constitutional link with Britain, was steadily gaining ground. The Home Rule movement was not separatist or republican; it sought a measure of Irish self-government under the British crown and it had the support of the Liberal Party from 1872.

It was the third Home Rule Bill of 1912 which was to be the test of wills between the Tories and the Liberals. The Liberals had passed the Parliament Act which curtailed the power of the Tory-dominated House of Lords. Before this the Lords had had the power to veto any act carried in the Commons. Now they could only delay a Bill or Act passed by the Commons. The Home Rule Bill became a rallying point for Tory discontent. Fearful of the consequences for the British class system if they organised against the Liberals on 'British' issues, they choose Ireland as the battlefield and Home Rule as the issue. They could not defeat democracy in Britain so they homed in on the anti-democratic spirit of Orangeism in North-East Ulster as a means of disrupting the advance towards democracy in Britain itself.

The main leadership of the opposition to Home Rule was provided by British Tories who now championed and instigated a reactionary movement in the north of Ireland. Tories rallied to the cause to defeat the 'tyranny of the commons' and provided the training and guns for the Ulster Volunteer Force (UVF) with the help of Sir Henry Wilson, Chief of the Imperial General Staff. Weapons were stored not only in Orange Halls in Belfast but in Tory clubs in Britain as well.

Inflammatory speeches by Tory leaders led to sectarian riots in Belfast and to attacks on Catholic workmen in Belfast shipyards, and as the temperature rose the UVF continued to arm itself. The Liberals did nothing to suppress this Tory conspiracy because of their fear of the fledgling British Labour movement. They reasoned that if they confronted the Tories the Labour Party would exploit the situation and encourage a class war in Britain, in which the Liberals as well as the Tories might perish. The climax of the Tory revolt occurred in 1914 when fifty-seven British army officers resigned after being ordered to put down the revolt, and this Curragh Mutiny broke the nerve of the Liberal Party.

The Home Rule Bill was suspended with the outbreak of the First World War but the forces of reaction which had been whipped up in the anti-Home Rule agitation commenced the process of institutionalising the sectarianism which they had encouraged. By this time Irish nationalist opinion had moved beyond Home Rule to the demand for an Irish Republic. When the First World War ended the creation of the Orange State with Sir Henry Wilson as chief military adviser and Sir Edward Carson as leader was well advanced. It was established in a frenzy of pogroms and sectarian attacks.

The Tory conspiracy succeeded, not only in Ireland where it interrupted and thwarted a struggle for national independence but in Britain also where reactionary notions still dominate many British working people. Although the British aristocracy is almost extinct the ideology of the aristocracy survives and the notion that some people — usually white people — are 'born to rule' lives on in an atmosphere of jingoism and chauvinism.

In Ireland the British partition institutionalised and provided a structure for such beliefs. Having established a 6 county state, the boundaries of which were designed to secure a permanent loyal majority, and having established a 'Protestant parliament for a Protestant people', the stability of the state and the maintenance of Protestant power required that a constant mentality of seige be maintained. This seige mentality was unconsciously described by Captain Terence O'Neill in an interview shortly after his resignation as Prime Minister:

> The basic fear of Protestants in Northern Ireland is that they will be outbred by the Roman Catholics. It is as simple as that.

Loyalism has attempted to project a conviction that certain qualities reside with 'us' and certain qualities with 'them', and such convictions have provided inherent justification for resisting the threat of Catholic equality. Particular Protestant qualities according to loyalism are perceived as being cleanliness, reliability, honesty, dedication, loyalty, respect for authority, thriftiness, respectability, and so on. Catholics, by and large, are perceived to lack such qualities. Thus if Catholics are allowed to 'get in everywhere' they will be bound to take advantage and to respond to the privilege afforded to them with duplicity and treachery. If they are given decent housing they will wreck it, if they are given jobs they will prove shiftless and work-shy; and so on. The litany would doubtless be utterly familiar in the southern United States, in European countries with migrant workforces, in South Africa and in Britain where the anti-Irish prejudices of the past have given way to anti-black prejudices of the same order.

While prejudice against Catholics was firmly entrenched centuries ago and became institutionalised in the 6 counties state, the expression of that prejudice was intensified in response to the civil rights movement and, even before that, in response to Unionist Prime Minister O'Neill's moves towards rapprochement with Dublin. As loyalists mobilised to attack civil rights marches, and as they launched pogroms to burn Catholics out of their homes, publication of sectarian songs and stories, old and new, flourished. Song with lyrics such as:

If guns were made for shooting,
Then skulls were made to crack.
You've never seen a better Taig
Than with a bullet in his back.

Later, the armed struggle of the IRA would be cited as justification, almost as if it were the source of loyalist prejudice. A letter in the February 1972 bulletin of the Ulster Defence Association (UDA) stated:

I have reached the stage where I no longer have any compassion for any nationalist, man, woman or child. After years of destruction, murder, intimidation, I have been driven against my better feelings to the decision — it's them or us ... Why have (loyalist paramilitaries) not started to hit back in the only way these nationalist bastards understand? That is, ruthless, indiscriminate killing ... If I had a flame-thrower I would roast the slimy excreta that pass for human beings.

The UDA replied: 'Without question most Protestants would agree with your sentiments. We do ....'

Most Protestants would most certainly not agree and it must also be said that there are many Protestants who are either quite free of prejudice or who, if they are in any way prejudiced nevertheless act in a completely unsectarian manner. However, in the 1980s in Belfast a loyalist local councillor enjoys popularity with his constituents after he suggested that Catholics should be incinerated. In the wake of the signing of the Hillsborough treaty Catholic churches, schools and houses have been attacked and ordinary Catholics have been assassinated, as in the past.

Loyalist politicians and others have suggested that the IRA

is engaged in a sectarian, anti-Protestant war, that it is carrying out a policy of genocide, particularly in border areas. The IRA has, over the years of its campaign, demonstrated an ability to carry out a massive bombing campaign against economic targets in the 6 counties, mortar and other attacks on RUC and British army barracks, attacks with bomb and bullet on the British army and on the state forces of the Ulster Defence Regiment (UDR), the RUC and prison warders. In the light of this demonstrated lethal ability and the experience acquired over the years, it is self-evident that if the IRA had wanted to launch attacks on the Protestant community it could have done so and inflicted unimaginable casualties. Presumably it would not be a major operation for the IRA to kill a hundred people on the Shankill Road tomorrow or to clear people off their small farms in country areas. If it is capable of mortaring heavily fortified British positions it could presumably deliberately inflict appalling civilian casualties. But it has not done that. And if it has not done it, then it must be because it does not want to, that it has decided that it does not want to engage in a war against the Protestant people.

It is sometimes said that the attacks on the UDR are seen by Protestants as attacks on the Protestant community. The shooting of an IRA volunteer may well be considered lamentable, but it will be seen simply as an attack on an IRA person. That small community in which the volunteer lived, if it is one of those communities that are constantly harassed by the RUC and UDR, might see it as an attack on one of their own, but no one will say that the volunteer was shot because he or she was a Catholic. Despite the public assertions of Unionist spokespersons they know that if there are five UDR men lined up by the IRA there is no question of asking which of these five are Protestant and which are Catholic.

Without wishing to dehumanise — because all these people are human beings — the identification with the forces of the state by one political section of the citizens of that state derives not so much because they see those forces as their co-religionists but because they see them as their armed forces, as the forces of Unionism, and it does not matter whether an RUC man or a UDR man is Protestant or Catholic. Attacks on the forces of the state are not attacks on the Protestant religion or the

Protestant community.

The major responsibility — and one can see this even in statements from Alan Wright of the RUC and in statements of some Protestant clergymen — for 'sectarianising' the conflict lies with the British government. They had 22,000 British soldiers in the 6 counties twelve years ago, but their NATO commitments and the political effects of casualties in Britain caused them to 'Ulsterise' the war. In this they engaged in a similar process to the one they employed in Cyprus with the consequence that they inflamed the differences between Turkish and Greek Cypriots; they picked their side there and they built a domestic force around it and that force was used against the other side. This process in Ireland has led to a primacy of the RUC and UDR, which have been pushed into the front line while the traditional British regiments have receded into the background, and that is why there has been an increase in casualties amongst the UDR and RUC. It is not that the IRA are singling out the RUC and UDR, because it would be safe to assume that the IRA, if they had a choice, would see a greater strategic importance in actions against the Parachute Regiment than, for example, against the Cullbacky UDR platoon.

Loyalists say they have problems about their religious liberties: that 'their' Protestant tradition is one which protects the freedom to practice one's religion, while the Roman Catholic tradition does not. There is a breathtaking nerve about such an assertion. Successive Protestant English administrations attempted to impose their faith upon the native Irish, to 'civilise the barbarians', and they failed. In the course of that failure they used the most draconian measures to outlaw and suppress catholicism, and in so doing they achieved a cementing of the relationship between the Catholic people and their church.

If one wishes to understand why Irish Catholics express in action such widespread allegiance to their church and their priests, then one must recognise the potency of the fact that people died for the right to worship, to practice their religion, to attend their own chapel.

The fact is that if one looks at the suppression of religious liberty in Ireland one finds ample and extreme evidence of it; but it is suppression by political Protestantism of Roman Catholicism and, for a period, the suppression by political

Protestantism of Presbyterianism. Republicans have always been dedicated to guaranteeing absolutely the right to religious and civil liberties. And it is worth noting that republicans have been and still are consistently condemned by a Catholic Hierarchy to a far greater extent than are Unionists. I have certainly been condemned more by Dr Daly Bishop of Down and Connor — not always by name but obviously by innuendo — than has Ian Paisley. There is no way that in terms of religious liberty either Protestants or Catholics have anything to fear from republicans. And there is no way that republicans, in pursuit of a secular or at least pluralist society, want to see any religious hierarchy given a position as of right as part of the state. Republicans want to limit the control of the churches to things spiritual and to treat everyone as equal before God.

It is undeniably the case that the 26 county state has been a confessional state since its inception, as has the 6 county state. Separated by partition from the very substantial Protestant minority on the island of Ireland, the 26 county state has contained only a relatively insignificant Protestant minority and has enacted and maintained social legislation which reflects the moral values of the church to which the vast majority of its citizens subscribe. Defenders of this pattern of social legislation and of the intervention of the Catholic hierarchy on such infamous occasions as the Mother and Child scheme controversy claim that the people of the 26 counties have democratically chosen social legislation permeated by a Catholic ethos.

But neither the 26 counties nor the 6 counties constitute democratically chosen units, and the consequences of imposed partition have been far more important than any conflict of historical perspectives. A Protestant national minority became a reactionary, sectarian majority in the 6 county statelet, and the national majority found its own particular conservative religious predilections virtually unchallenged within the 26 county statelet. Partition has, as Connolly foresaw, created a 'carnival of reaction' on both sides of the border.

Loyalists protest that republicans propose their absorption into the 26 county state. I would not insult anyone by asking them to join a 32 county state based upon the present 26 county model or by offering it, or any aspect of it, as a blueprint. But when Unionist politicians condemn the 26 counties — as, for example,

Bob McCartney has — for being a confessional state, I have to ask why he is doing nothing about his own state.

Republicans do not propose the amalgamation of the two statelets into a 32 county Free State. What republicans are talking about is political representatives of Irish people sitting down without outside interference and deciding what kind of society suits all our interests. I happen to support, although I am a Catholic, the creation of a secular society, a society which is run in the interests of all its citizens, a pluralist society which is structured in such a way as to reflect differing traditions and which is shaped by the aspirations of all its citizens. In other words a state which would 'unite the whole people of Ireland, to abolish the memory of past dissensions and to substitute the common name of Irish person in place of the denominations of Protestant, Catholic and Dissenter. . .'

What republicanism has to offer loyalists is equality. We propose deciding together what can be done about the real problems of the people and doing so within a legislature which actually represents those people, which reflects their needs, which guarantees their liberties and which has no vested interest in disadvantaging anyone.

Republicans say these kinds of things quite often but they are not going to be listened to while partition remains because there is no political force in the world which suddenly wakes up, perceives it has been wrong and then goes about rectifying the situation. The hard reality of it is that people meet new situations pragmatically, and there is plenty of history of that. The Unionists were opposed to Home Rule — they accepted Home Rule; they were opposed to partition — they accepted a 6 county state; they would not allow the disbanding of the 'B' Specials — they accepted the disbanding of the 'B' Specials; Stormont was to be fiercely maintained — it was prorogued.

I have had no amicable discussions with senior loyalist politicians; but I have met — in prisons and out of prisons, and even formally — a number of minor loyalist politicians and representatives of loyalist paramilitary groupings. My perception of them is that they are concerned to fight their own sectarian corner and they see no reason to stop doing that while the Union with Britain still holds. Once that changes, once their corner is no longer defined by the British presence, then I think that it becomes a matter of businesslike negotiation. I have no wish to gloss over or minimise the difficulties, but it is basically a matter of Irish democrats being markedly unsectarian but dogmatically and unapologetically democratic. Loyalists can have no significant say under British rule and they should have no veto on the British connection, but they can have and should have a very big say in the shape of an independent Irish constitution and in the shape of an independent Irish society.

Loyalism required a one-party state, and this required the exclusion of non-loyalists. Republicans desire a democratic society, and this requires the full involvement of everyone. The only way in which we can live together peacefully is in a situation where we are all equal. We cannot be equal in the 6 county state: the very nature and history of the state proves that. We cannot be equal in terms of our relations with Britain because all of us, despite our political differences, are treated as second or third-class citizens within the United Kingdom. The only context in which we can have equality is where we are in control of our own destiny.

The loyalist veto is utterly undemocratic both in the Irish and British context. If the majority of the people in the United Kingdom, of which the 6 county state is supposed to be a part, decided they wanted to end the Union, the veto says they could not. It is undemocratic in terms of Ireland where clearly a majority of the people on the island would like to break the connection with Britain. The reassurance given to the Protestant ascendancy has been restated once more in the Hillsborough treaty. Indeed, it has been more than restated because now the London government can say not only that the majority of people in 'the province', as they call it, want the Union, they can also say that the Dublin government also supports the loyalist veto. And Tom King, the British Minister for 'Northern Ireland', can say that the agreement guarantees that there can never be a united Ireland.

The loyalists have a desperate identity crisis. They agonise over whether they are Ulster-Scotch, Picts, English or British. When they go to England they are Paddies. They express a massive rejection of a very rich Irish culture, despite the fact that this heritage cannot in any way reasonably be regarded as exclusive. Instead they waste their time trying to work out some kind of obscure notion of Ulster Protestant culture. They reject Irish music, the Irish language, Irish dance, Irish history, a whole culture which should be theirs and which would be even richer for their participation in it. Yet they are not British. Loyalism is not found in Britain itself except as an Irish export. There are no cultural or national links between the loyalists and the British, no matter how much the loyalists scream about their 'British way of life'. The British today are embarrassed by the vulgarity of loyalism and, as republicans have consistently warned over the last fifteen years, would dump the loyalists if they thought they could find a more stable and internationally acceptable ally in Ireland.

The loyalists are Irish and the notion that they have of being exclusively British is a comparatively recent one. They are Irish people who wish to be subjects of the British crown for as long as that crown protects the Orange ascendancy. Before partition all loyalists regarded themselves without question as being Irish, except that they were the loyal sort of Irish. It was only when revolutionary nationalism threatened the British Empire, upon which loyalism depended, that Ireland became repugnant as a nation because it would not co-operate passively with British interests.

This attitude was reinforced by partition when the Irish identity was allowed to become synonymous with Catholicism, disloyalty, republicanism and anything else which was imagined to be a threat to the Protestant ascendancy.

In recent times sections of the loyalist community have been promoting the idea of repartition, of 'independence' or of re-negotiating the Union as a means of safeguarding their power base or as they, with unconscious irony, put it, 'safeguarding the British way of life'. Their loyalty is conditional and their 'patriotic' focus can change according to the political circumstances.

Loyalist paramilitary leaders frequently boast that I and other prominent republicans are on the top of their list for assassination, and many innocent Catholics have been murdered by organisations whose leaders have made careers out of sectarianism. I and a number of comrades were wounded in one loyalist attack, yet I feel no hatred towards those who are trying to kill us. They are doing their duty as they see it and are unfortunate dupes of salaried politicians and victims of colonialism.

While I am dogmatic and unapologetic in my opposition to the loyalist veto, one can at the same time be compassionate and understand that it is only when the British colonial prop which creates sectarian division is removed that Protestants will be able to embrace, enrich and enjoy a heritage which is in a very real sense theirs as much as it is anyone else's. God speed the day.

A new electoral map of the North

May 1985 — Local Government Elections in the North

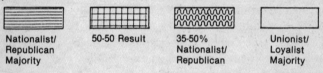

Nationalist/ Republican Majority   50-50 Result   35-50% Nationalist/ Republican   Unionist/ Loyalist Majority

A new electoral map of Ireland

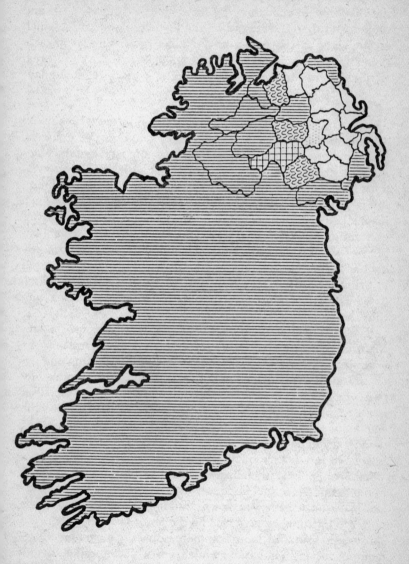

Republicanism and Socialism

The cause of Labour is the cause of Ireland.
The cause of Ireland is the cause of Labour.
James Connolly

IF YOU WANT to talk about socialism in the Irish context you cannot divorce the socialist aspiration from the aspiration of national independence. This is the big lesson of the Connolly experience. In order to bring about a socialist society you must have real national independence. To use Connolly's phrase, this requires the reconquest of Ireland by the Irish people, which means the expulsion of imperialism in all its forms, political, economic, military, social and cultural. It means the establishment of a real Irish republic and the organisation of the economy so that all its resources are under Irish control and organised to bring maximum benefit to our people in a 32 county state in which Irish culture and national identity are strong and confident.

Real national independence is the pre-requisite of socialism. My understanding of socialism is that it is a definite form of society in which the main means of production, distribution and exchange are socially owned and controlled and in which production is based on human need rather than private profit. Socialism is based on the most thorough-going democratisation of the economic system, side by side with the most thorough-going democracy in politics and public affairs. Socialism includes and is a stage in advance of republicanism.

You cannot have socialism in a British colony, such as exists in the 6 counties or in a neo-colony such as exists in the 26 counties. You must have your own national government with the power to institute the political and economic changes which constitute socialism. Furthermore, there cannot be a credible movement for socialism in Ireland while the British connection divides workers in the 6 counties and while partition prevents a unity of working class interests. One does not become a socialist merely by calling oneself that. After all, Hitler's fascist movement called itself National Socialists, the Nazis. Today such politicians as Neil Kinnock, Roy Mason, Harold Wilson, Fidel Castro, Yasser Arafat and Mikhail Gorbachev call themselves socialists. Nearer home John Hume, Tomás Mac Giolla, Dick Spring and Michael O'Riordan call themselves socialists also. Clearly socialism is what socialism does. It means different things to different people and nothing to most people and is second only to republicanism as the most abused political description in Irish politics.

The acid test of commitment to socialism in Ireland (and Britain as well) is to be found in one's attitude to the issue of Irish national self-determination. The correct socialist attitude to Ireland must be an internationalist one. You cannot be a socialist without being a separatist. You cannot be a socialist if you condone, support or ignore the colonial stranglehold which the British government maintains over this part of our country. There cannot be such a thing as 'Ulster Socialism'. Those who profess to be 'Northern Ireland Socialists' are involved in mere parochialism of the gasworks and waterworks municipal variety. Neither does one become socialist by abandoning nationalism and republicanism and replacing them with 'leftist' sloganising like the Workers' Party or by becoming anti-national like the Irish Labour Party. Those who seek affiliation with British socialist parties are bowing to or blinding themselves to the colonial nature of the relationship between Britain and Ireland and they ignore the geographical, national and cultural differences between us. The relationship between socialists in Ireland and Britain should be a relationship of equals.

There are other 'international' socialists who support the legitimate rights of the people of Central America, Africa, the Middle East and elsewhere to engage in struggles for national freedom. They are hypocrites if they do not assert the same rights for the Irish people.

The Irish nationalist movement played a leading role in the development of the world-wide struggle to overthrow colonialism and throughout its history republicanism has been strongly influenced by progressive movements in other countries. The ideas of the American War of Independence and the French Revolution were those which inspired the United Irishmen. Irish emigrants played a leading role in the American War of Independence and in the struggle against Portugese and Spanish colonialism in Central and South America. In India and Africa the Irish revolutionary tradition was one of the strongest influences in the anti-colonial movements. Even in Britain the Chartist movement and the whole development of British trade unionism owed much to leadership from Irish radicals.

In more recent times internationalism has been an important element in republicanism, both in terms of the tactics of guerrilla war and the development of political ideas. Republicans have learnt from struggles in other countries and movements in many countries have acknowledged a debt to Irish republicanism. Most guerrilla movements study the IRA and its mode of struggle and see it as a major example of how to develop a people's war. In the post-colonial era the emergence of successful struggles internationally has had a substantial effect on republicans. There is a natural affinity and there is therefore an openness to the ideas associated with these struggles.

The 'network of terror' propaganda put out by the likes of the Monday Club in Britain or in newspapers, books and magazines from the USA, by pet journalists of the CIA in particular, is a deliberate attempt to misrepresent our internationalist position. One of the ways in which this is done is by associating the republican movement with the actions of groups such as the Red Brigade, the Red Army Faction/Baader-Meinhoff and Direct Action, despite the fact that at successive Árd Fheiseanna Sinn Féin has denounced the actions of such groups.

Certain liberals and self-proclaimed socialists who are implacably opposed to the struggle for independence in their own country nevertheless profess a kind of internationalism which engages in long-distance support for revolutionary movements, provided of course that their struggles are in other countries. John Hume, for example, is a sponsor of the anti-apartheid movement, as was Garrett FitzGerald until recently. The anti-apartheid movement supports the right of the African National Congress (ANC) to pursue its aims by means of armed struggle. John Hume and Garret FitzGerald's views on a similar struggle in Ireland are well known, as are those of Neil Kinnock who applauded and embraced Oliver Tambo, President of the ANC at the British Labour Party Conference when Tambo spelt out the need for an intensification of the armed struggle and the probability of civilian casualties.

Irish republicans, on the other hand, have a natural, instinctive and deep affinity with the ANC and with the black majority who are oppressed in South Africa. The appearance of solidarity slogans or vividly painted murals on gable walls throughout the nationalist ghettoes of the 6 counties is but one example of this identification with liberation struggles throughout the world. The indignation of ordinary nationalists in the 6 counties at Reagan's attempts to bully or undermine the government of Nicaragua, and their obvious sorrow at the forced eviction of the PLO from Beirut, provide ample evidence of the strength of their anti-imperialist and internationalist instincts.

All socialists must be internationalists and anti-imperialists in a meaningful way. Long distance 'revolutionaries' will not help to free the oppressed peoples of the world if they cannot help to free their own people and class in Ireland.

A free federation of free peoples is the only conception of internationalism worth struggling for. So socialists must struggle for freedom and political power in the country in which they live and give a lead to struggling people elsewhere.

For all these reasons and because I am a socialist I continue to be a republican. Republicanism is a philosophy in which the national and the radical social dimensions are the two sides of the one coin. While the national dimensions has, for historical reasons, been the most dominant tendency within the republican movement, Irish republicanism has consistently been a radical political philosophy. Republicans have persistently, against great odds and often alone, struggled against imperialism. The republican movement has many inadequacies but it remains the major, many would say the only, anti-imperialist force in Ireland today. The advance from today's situation into national independence as defined by Irish republicanism places socialism on the agenda but Irish republicanism is not a term which defines a system of society in the way that socialism does. In our case it refers to the aim of securing national independence in its broadest sense. Despite the best efforts of the Fianna Fáil, SDLP and Fine Gael leaderships to distort its meaning republicanism is a concept easily understood by the majority of Irish people to mean national independence, unity, sovereignty and an end to foreign interference in our affairs.

You cannot be a socialist and not be a republican. Socialists will want an independent republic because it is a good thing in itself as an advance from today's situation and because it is an essential step towards socialism. This will only be achieved, however, if the struggle is led by the most radical social groups and in particular by the working class — without whom it cannot succeed in developing the conditions for the establishment of a democratic and socialist state.

Such a struggle for national independence needs to encompass all the social elements in the nation which are oppressed or held back by imperialism. Independence struggles which are led by the conservative or middle classes, as in Ireland in 1921, tend to compromise with imperialism because their leading sections benefit from such a compromise. That is why those on the left in Ireland who regard themselves as socialists and as representing the working class should be the most uncompromising republicans.

In all of this the question of socialist republicanism or republican socialism is an important one for radicals in Ireland today. The term 'republican socialism' has been used by some, for example the now almost defunct IRSP; but strictly speaking it is a misnomer. If you say you are a republican socialist you are implying that there is such a thing as a 'non-republican' socialist; but of course there is not and cannot be, at least if socialism is used in the classical sense of the term defined here. One cannot be a socialist and not be a republican. Connolly, as usual, indicated what the correct term was when he called the party he founded in 1896 the Irish Socialist Republican Party. It follows that if a republican wishes to use the term 'socialist' in defining his or her political position today, the proper term is 'socialist republican' and 'socialist republicanism', in order to distinguish oneself from non-socialist republicans. This is perfectly valid. However, the republican struggle should not at this stage of its development style itself 'socialist-republican'. This would imply that there is no place in it for non-socialists.

There are a number of 'isms' involved in Irish republicanism; combined they make the one great 'ism' of Irish republicanism. Omit one or more and you have a different philosophy. Five related elements are separatism, secularism, anti-sectarianism, nationalism and the radical social dimension. But Irish republicanism is not and never has been a static concept; it is a living and developing ideology. The finest declaration of its principal elements is contained in the 1916 Proclamation, which has pride of place in many Irish homes. Unfortunately, it is rarely studied and its content is deliberately downgraded by the Dublin establishment whose main parties nevertheless claim to base their policies on this unique declaration of social and democratic intent.

Irish republicanism, greatly influenced by the French revolution, was first articulated by the United Irishmen and in particular by Wolfe Tone, whose writings detail the bases of republicanism in his time. These were separatism: to break the connection with England; non-sectarianism: to substitute the common name of Irish person in place of Protestant, Catholic and Dissenter; and secularism. Later, with the emergence of the Young Ireland movement Fintan Lalor gave Irish republicanism a new base. He wrote:

The entire ownership of Ireland moral and material, up to the sun and down to the centre, is vested in the right of the people of Ireland. They and none but they are the land-owners and law makers of this island, that all laws are null and void not made by them and all titles to land are invalid not conferred by them.

The Young Irelanders also reawakened a sense of national consciousness and awareness of national identity.

The next influence was the Irish Republican Brotherhood, or the Fenian movement, whose rise accompanied a great national revival and the foundation of national sporting and cultural organisations such as the GAA and Conradh na Gaeilge. This nationalism was not chauvinist — it was not the nationalism of imperialism — but was a progressive nationalism expressing a belief in culture and identity as well as in political independence.

Although there was a progressive social element in the writings of all the generations that have influenced Irish republicanism, and although in their own time these were radical revolutionary movements, James Connolly's writings on the social and economic aspects of the struggle for Irish independence were to have the most significant effect not only in its literature but on the thoughts of the other leaders. Padraig Pearse's *The Sovereign People* provides a sample of this:

> So that the nation's sovereignty extends not only to all men and women of the nation but to all material possessions of the nation, the nation's soil and all its resources, all wealth and all wealth producing processes within the nation. In other words, no private right to property is good against the public right to secure strictly equal rights and liberties to every man and woman within the nation.

All of these elements were crystallised in the Proclamation of the Republic in 1916 and developed further in the Democratic Programme of the First Dáil. These documents have neither been implemented nor updated to meet modern conditions, yet they are as relevant today as they were when their basic principals were conceived.

All of the movements and leaders that shaped the republican philosophy were also internationalist in outlook and considered and engaged in physical force as a means of advancing the struggle. If we compare the political positions of those politicians and political parties that pretend to be republican with all the elements of Irish republicanism we discover how shoddy and superficial their pretence actually is.

Unless one embraces all of the 'isms' of republicanism one cannot be a republican. That is not to say that those who may not agree with every 'ism' have no part to play in this phase of the struggle. On the contrary, agreement on one element leading to an involvement in struggle for the achievement of agreed *short-term* objectives is desirable, but republicans — those who embrace all the 'isms' — should always be in the vanguard and should have the ability to shape our struggle so that it draws the maximum support from all progressive and oppressed elements in Irish society today.

In Ireland until partition is got rid of and a united Ireland established, being genuinely left-wing is to be an out-and-out republican. This was the key lesson of James Connolly for socialists in Ireland. That is why he was led, as a socialist, to join Pearse and the other radical republicans and democrats in a fight to establish an Irish Republic.

If that fight had been successful, Connolly and the socialists would then have been in the best position to advocate the economic and social changes which constitute socialism. They would have proved themselves by their leadership of the independence struggle. That is why it is a political mistake to counterpose republicanism and socialism in Ireland as if they were opposites or antagonistic.

The true socialist will be an active supporter of the republican character of the national independence movement. She or he will realise that unless this character is maintained and unless the most radical social forces are in the leadership of the independence struggle then inevitably it must fail or compromise. This classical view of the matter contrasts with the ultra-left view, which counterposes republicanism and socialism and which breaks up the unity of the national independence movement by putting forward 'socialist' demands that have no possibility of being achieved until real independence is won; the result is that one gets neither independence nor socialism.

To ignore these lessons of history is to repeat the mistakes of the past. What is needed in Ireland, especially in the 26 counties, is the development of an anti-imperialist movement. Such a movement cannot be built around the slogan of socialism until socialism comes on the historical agenda, until a distinctly Irish form of socialism is developed to meet our needs and conditions and until the majority class in Ireland, the working class, actually understands that this is in their interests and is what they want.

If such a mass anti-imperialist movement, with an appeal to all major sections of Irish society, could be developed, and this is the urgent task of all socialists, nationalists and republicans, it would fuse together all those whose interests are adversely affected by imperialism and would show people the connection between their localised and special grievances and the imperialistic domination of Irish society.

The programme for such a movement would appeal to all those capable of taking a national stand and would require a multi-sided campaign of national regeneration — a new Irish-Ireland movement to offset, especially in the 26 counties, the neo-colonial ethos and anti-national mentality which exists there. And such a programme would, by its very nature, be to the left of what passes for 'socialism' in Ireland today.

Connolly held that the national revolution was the pre-requisite of the socialist revolution. All of us who profess to be republicans or socialists would do well to study his writings. As Desmond Greaves has written, Connolly held that the political and economic aspects are the two stages of one democratic reorganisation of society, each involving economic changes which it is the function of political change to promote. We who attempt to follow in his tradition must recognise that truth.

Culture

Mise Éire!
Is sine mé ná an Chailleach Béara!
Mór mo ghlóir!
Mé do rug Cú Chullain cróga!
Mór mo náire!
Mo chlann féin do dhíol a máthair!
Mise Éire!
Is uaigní mé ná an Chailleach Béara!

AT A RECENT Sinn Féin slógadh one speaker questioned the use of the term cultural to describe our political offensives on the question of language and national consciousness. This speaker held that culture is seen by many people to have something to do with ballet dancing. His point was well taken. Culture is a term with a wide variety of meanings and is understood in many different ways. Some people associate it with art, opera, classical music; others with the theatre or classical literature. In other words, it is often perceived as a high-brow commodity consisting of certain activities which are seen as the preserve of a privileged minority.

Culture is not, of course, the preserve of any one set of people or of any one class. Culture involves every aspect of our lives and is not restricted to the artistic expressions which humankind has developed. Culture is the ideas and attitudes of people; it is an indication of how we view things and it is our response to the environment in which we live. National culture is the reflection of the politics, economics, values, attitudes, aspirations and thoughts of a nation. It is the totality of our response to the world we live in.

Precisely because this is so, cultural colonialism formed and forms a major part of the conquest of Ireland. As Pearse wrote in *The Murder Machine:*

The system has aimed at the substitution for men and women of mere things. . . Things have no allegiance. Like other things they are for sale. . . There is no education system in Ireland. The English have established the simulacrum of an educational system but its object is the precise contrary of the object of an education system. Education should foster; this education is meant to repress. Education should inspire; this education is meant to tame. Education should harden; this education is meant to enervate. The English are too wise a people to educate the Irish, in any worthy sense. As well expect them to arm us.

Pearse's observations are as relevant today as they were when they were written. An educational system which taught people to question their society, their environment, their social or economic disadvantage, an educational system which assisted people to strive for the common good, to form and voice radical opinions, to seek change, would do no service to those in control of the social and economic order in Ireland today. 'As well expect them to arm us.' Instead our educational system instils the values of materialism, of the profit motive. It teaches the ways of colonialism, the values of imperialism and survivalism and eradicates our sense of national culture, of independence, of individualism.

A national system of education was introduced to Ireland by the English ruling class before it was introduced in England. Its purpose was to break the national consciousness of the Irish people, to 'civilise the barbarians' by the methods later used throughout the world for the same purpose by all major powers.

There is no such thing as a neutral language, for language is the means by which culture, the totality of our response to the world we live in, is communicated; and for that reason the Irish language had to be destroyed. When a people have spoken a common language for thousands of years that language reflects their history, sentiments, outlook and philosophy. Culture is filtered through it and when the language is lost everything it represents is also lost. The Irish language has more than 2,000 years of unbroken history in Ireland. Apart from Greek, Irish has the oldest literature of any living European language. It is a badge of a civilisation whose values were vastly different from the one which seeks to subjugate us. It is a badge of our identity and part of what we are. If we were to be made little Englanders, that badge had to be removed, that culture destroyed and that civilisation replaced by an order which accommodated and acquiesced to the interests of our new rulers.

The Gaelic social system in Ireland was communal. A substantial part of the land was common land and although individuals could own land they could not dispose of it as they pleased — outside the clan or sept, for example. Even cattle could not be disposed of by the individual without the consent of the clan. Chiefs were elected, usually from a single family, but there was no such concept as primogeniture. A woman could be elected as chief and the electoral system and chieftainship often passed through the female line, as exemplified in the ancient sagas of the Ulster Cycle. The basis of early Irish law, known as the Brehon laws and first codified in the 5th Century AD, was arbitration and compensation, and under the law there was a custom of ritual fasting as a method of asserting one's rights if the person who had inflicted injury was reluctant to accept arbitration.

Few of the great ancient civilisations made any provision for the poor who were sick. The Buddhists of Eastern India and the Irish were the two notable exceptions. In 300 BC a hospital was established near Ard Macha (Armagh); each clan had its own bruidhean or public hostel where, free of charge, travellers were provided with shelter and hospitality. The *Senchas Mór* and the *Book of Aicill* are explicit on the rights of the sick and 'welfare state' provisions to offset the economic consequences of sickness and old age. The Gaelic educational system and the honoured position of the bards both show how emphasis was placed on improving the intellect, on creating and maintaining an ethos in which learning in its true sense flourished.

I outline the above not because we seek to go back to those days or to that existence but in order to sketch a brief outline of the kind of civilisation which had to be destroyed to make the conquest possible. It also illustrates usefully the fact that it is capitalistic ideas, feudalism and the concept of private property which have been imported into Ireland, not socialist ideas. That many people believe the opposite is but one example of how the revision of history has succeeded.

We do not seek to recover the past but to discover it so that we can recover the best of our traditional values and mould them to the present. Our national culture should reflect the combination of the different influences within the nation: urban and rural, Gaeltacht and Galltacht, northern and southern, orange and green. The revival of the Irish language as the badge of identity, as a component part of our culture and as the filter through which it is expressed, is a central aspect of the reconquest.

Loyalist leaders today attack Irish culture and particularly the language as being non-Protestant. This is a nonsense, but the reasons for their hostility are obvious enough: for the Protestant people to embrace the Irish language today would be for them to reject loyalism.

Until 1601 and the defeat at Kinsale our culture, shared by all our people, was dominant throughout this island and even until the great starvation of the 1840s Irish was the spoken language of the majority of the people. It has only ceased to be so in the last 150 to 100 years. The anglicisation process was a long and cruel one and has never been totally successful. Even when the people were dispossessed and the independent aristocratic Gaelic culture destroyed with the Flight of the Earls and the great plantations, the hidden Ireland lived on as the culture of an oppressed people.

Its decline can be dated to a modernisation of the relationship between England and Ireland, the Act of Union, after which the emerging middle class, unlike the Gaelic aristocracy who patronised the bards and harpers, strongly rejected the Irish language and customs. They had embraced the new order and rejected the old values. To succeed meant speaking English, rising above the herd. To be Irish was to be ignorant.

The emerging Irish establishment, including the Catholic church, which had up to that time been a source of some strength to the common people, succeeded where the 'bata scóir', the enforcement of the English language on children and the need for English in the market place had failed. Even when they fled to 'Hell or Connaught' the people took their culture with them. But now social and economic advancement became synonymous with the use of English language, mannerisms and culture.

This process has been refined in modern Ireland and the native administration in the 26 counties in particular stands indicted on this score. Irish still remains the official first language yet only two per cent of state broadcasting is in the Irish language and the last bastions of the language, the Gaeltachtaí, are being steadily eroded as a result of a deliberate policy by the state.

Numerous reports chart the decline of the Gaeltachtaí, which have suffered a faster rate of depopulation in the last twenty years than at any time in the past century. The main reason is a particularly high rate of out-migration accounting for two out of every three people born in the areas. In most cases it is the better educated and younger people who go, leaving behind a population with a severe imbalance in many of its structural features. The combination of fewer young people and more old people has meant a low rate of natural increase.

The Gaeltachtaí are dwindling, as is the amount of Irish spoken in them. In West Donegal, which I have visited regularly since my schooldays, one now has to go further into the Gaeltacht than previously. The Galltacht is encroaching on what were once Irish-speaking areas. Many children are now being raised in English where only fifteen or twenty years ago Irish was their first language. With the lack of economic, social and industrial infrastructure the parents know that their children must leave home to find employment. The parents have fallen into the habit of speaking English and their children follow suit. Indeed, it is a miracle that any vestige of Irish culture or way of life remains.

Cultural colonialism demands today, as it did in the past, the lowering of national spirit, the revision of history and the destruction of our separate identity. Our cultural identity and our language would act as a counter or, in MacSwiney's words, as 'the frontier' against our submergence by a West British, shoneen ethos or by a rampant Anglo-American 'Rambo' ethos. If we are to accept our lot as a poor, partitioned off-shore island, if we are to be obedient to the dictates of the nuclear powers, the directives from Brussels; if our rulers are to be free to collaborate with the British in governing part of our country as a British possession; even if we are to accept emigration or the dangers caused by Sellafield, then we must be conditioned to become 'mere things' because 'things have no allegiance'. In the Ireland of today our culture must not be *our* ideas and *our* attitudes. It must not be *our* view of things or *our* response to the environment we live in. It must instead be a reflection of the survivalism engendered by centuries of British colonialist and imperialist oppression. In other words, it must be the reflection of the politics, economics, values, attitudes, aspirations and thoughts of our rulers.

Garret FitzGerald's toadyism is a reflection of this dependency culture. Irish people cringed when he replied in English to a question in Irish at a press conference in Chequers. Later I had the opportunity to contrast his behaviour with the attitude of a foreign administration, at the extradition hearing of Gerry Kelly and Brendan MacFarlane in Amsterdam, where English is gaining primacy. The hearing was in Dutch and translated into English not, as the President of the court explained, 'because we don't understand English but because Dutch is our language'. Irish people were to cringe even more when FitzGerald as 'their leader' left the country on St. Patrick's Day to be televised sharing a 'begorrah' with Ronald Reagan, together with a jar of green jellybeans and a midget dressed up as a leprechaun.

This dependency culture expresses itself in both parts of Ireland today in resistance to change, in a lack of national pride, a feeling of national inferiority and in begrudgery. As Samuel Johnson observed, 'The Irish are a fair people. They never speak well of each other.' And why should they? We have been taught for 800 years not to.

Chief Psychiatrist of the Eastern Health Board, Dr Ivor Browne, has written:

> Our past as a nation has been so crushing and so painful that we are too inclined to rush blindly ahead and leave it behind us. The fact is that we cannot go ahead in any real sense unless we identify where we are in relation to where we have been. If, as a society, we cannot take hold of ourselves so as to be effective in the running of our affairs and the management of our economy, and if we adopt a relationship of dependency to other countries and outside economic forces, then is it any wonder that the individual can find no place or room to act; that when in this country someone comes up with a creative idea, all those around him set themselves energetically to the task of denigrating that idea, of finding reasons why it could not work.

The culture being forced through most of Irish society today is a dependency culture not only in the 26 counties but in the 6 counties as well; it affects loyalists as much as it affects citizens of the 26 counties. This dependency culture is based on escapism and plays its role in conditioning people to the acceptance of bad housing, unemployment, emigration, rising prices and falling living standards, bigotry, violence and a 'no hope' future.

Loyalist leaders who express hostility to the Irish language are actually denying their own past. Not only is this past evident in many of their names (for example McCusker and Maginnis), it is obvious also in the fact that at the time of the siege of Derry most of the population spoke Irish. Indeed, Irish Protestants in the late eighteenth century showed considerable interest in Irish music, literature and language.

In the liberal era of the 1790s the Belfast Harp Society flourished, the Belfast Reading Society (now the Linen Hall Library) was in the vanguard of the Irish revival, and the *Northern Star* published an Irish-language magazine, *Bolg an tSolar*. Belfast Acadmy had an Irish teacher and pupils there, like the patrons of the Reading Society and the Harp Society and the readers of the *Northern Star*, were mainly Protestants. Despite the sectarianism which replaced this liberal ethos An Cuideacht Gaedhilge Uladh (Ulster Gaelic Society) was founded in 1830 by two wealthy Protestants, Robert MacAdam and Lord Devonshire. MacAdam's sterling work in the promotion and recording of the Irish language is described in Brendan Ó Buachalla's *I mBéal Feirste Cois Cuin*.

While this interest amongst Protestants was to decline, the goodwill towards the language among patriotic Protestants continued. Douglas Hyde was to become one of the founders of the Gaelic League in 1893 and in the early 1900s the northern revival was led by other Protestants, such as Francis Biggar and Alice Milligan, founder of *An Shan Van Vocht*.

* * *

The struggle against cultural colonialism must be a key part of the reconquest of Ireland, of the making of a new Irish humanity. As we have seen, this does not mean going backwards. Neither does it mean merely preserving our language or our culture. Some people talk about 'preserving' the language: it is as if it was something to be kept as an archaic object to be brought out occasionally and shown to tourists. It is a notion of 'jam-jar' Irish. My own conviction is that the restoration of our culture must be a crucial part of our political struggle and that the restoration of the Irish language must be a central part of the cultural struggle. Culture is too important to be left to the cultural specialists. I agree with the late Máirtín Ó Cadhain, IRA activist, professor and writer, when he said, 'Tosóidh athghabháil na hÉireann le hathghabháil na Gaeilge.' (*The reconquest of Ireland will begin with the reconquest of the Irish language*.)

Steve Biko, the murdered black Southern African leader said, 'The greatest weapon in the hands of the oppressor is the mind of the oppressed.' In this regard I feel that many northern nationalists and republicans are much freer than their fellow Irish citizens in the 26 counties. Our minds are free: this is a truth which is understood by the imperial powers and their allies in Dublin and it is the main reason why there has been a recent revival in Irish culture in the six counties and a corresponding attempt to divert this by way of petty legislation promised by the Hillsborough treaty. As the British Minister responsible, Richard Needham, observed in a confidential letter,

> I gather that the Irish [Dublin government] place heavy significance on early progress in removing the prohibition on the use of any language other than English in street signs. Apparently they consider that this would help to reduce the publicity and support which Sinn Fein has obtained through the use of street signs in Irish. The Irish [Dublin government] are accordingly pressing strongly for us to publish in the Autumn proposals for a draft Order.

In the late '60s the civil rights struggle provided a broad enough appeal to bring out a substantial proportion of the anti-imperialist population. The activists of the Irish language movement had until then ploughed a lonely furrow but the repression directed against the civil rights struggle, followed by internment, re-awakened a consciousness about our language and culture. As the struggle has continued it has been accompanied by an increasing depth in the ideology of the people and a reinvigoration of our culture in all its forms.

As Padraig Ó Maolcraoibhe records,

> When the men in the H-Blocks of Long Kesh and the women in Armagh prison were stripped of everything they discovered that they could not be stripped of their language. It became

a means of resistance, of asserting their dignity and identity. In the H-Blocks, with no books, no paper, no pens, no professional teachers, young men living in filthy conditions, frequently beaten, stripped naked ... but unbowed, taught each other Irish by shouting lessons from cell to cell. And as one hunger strike was followed by the other the people outside learned these lessons also and they determined to carry on the cultural struggle — each one from where s/he was.

There is nothing trivial or folksy in the present interest of northern nationalists in the Irish language and these positive attitudes do not exist only in the 6 counties but they predominate there. In Belfast there has been a considerable revival in the use of Irish and the particular significance of this is that it is the first time it has ever happened within a working class community.

In practice this revival is expressed in small ways, with language classes in social clubs, with all-Irish nursery schools, with the Gaelicisation of street names. As a result one finds young people with Doctor Martin boots, knee-high denims and punk hairstyles peppering their talk with Irish phrases. Rough as it may be it represents culture in a living sense. It is 'survival' Irish, which enables people to exchange greetings and have some basic conversations. There is an all-Irish daily paper, *Lá*, published in Belfast, the first ever daily newspaper in any Celtic language. In West Belfast there are more than 60 adult Irish classes, but the greatest hope lies in the growth of education through the medium of Irish.

In 1970 there were no schools in the 6 counties in which education was through Irish. Scoil Phobal Feirste opened in West Belfast as an all-Irish primary school with nine pupils in 1971. By 1977 it was still the only school in the 6 counties, with just 30 pupils and two teachers. By May 1986 it had 194 pupils and nine teachers, plus a nursery school with 120 pupils. There are now also four other nursery schools in Belfast and three in Derry as well as two all-Irish streams in a County Derry primary school at Steelestown.

In 1977 there were 22 all-Irish nursery schools in the whole of Ireland. Today there are 150. In the 1981 census in the 26 counties a million people said they knew some Irish. This is the highest number of people knowing Irish in the past hundred years. Modern Gaelic literature is showing a remarkable resilience and vigour and there is now a new national Sunday newspaper, *Anois*, for the first time; since January 1986 Sinn Féin has produced *Nuacht Feirste*, a weekly newspaper in Irish.

There is without doubt a goodwill among the common people towards the language. And this is not confined to the north. In every survey carried out in the 26 counties the great majority of people there have declared that they are in favour of more being done to increase the use of Irish. It is interesting to note that a recent survey commissioned by the Irish National Teachers Organisation and carried out by MRBI shows that the working class and the lower middle class and the farming community as a whole are more favourable to the Irish language and to every other aspect of Irish culture than the middle and upper middle classes.

Culture is not a party political question or the monopoly of any one section of the people, but the destruction of our culture was a political act and its revival also requires political action. No progress can be made in any political struggle without the involvement of ordinary people, and the most pertinent point about the current modest revival is that it is happening because the ordinary people have identified with it.

Revolutionary republicans must come to understand the centrality of cultural resistance in the struggle for the reconquest of Ireland. As Pádraig Pearse said of the Gaelic League, the Easter Rising of 1916 was assured from the moment the League was founded. For their part Irish language enthusiasts who think that the language can be fully restored without national independence must listen to the voice of Ó Cadhain when he tells us,

> Ní hé amháin gur chóir do lucht na Gaeilge a bheith páirteach i gcogadh seo athghabhála na hÉireann — is é an t-aon rud é ar fiú a bheith páirteach ann in Éirinn — ach is é ár ndualgas a bheith dhá chinnireacht agus dhá threorú. Bíodh an Ghaeilge ag stiúra na réabhlóide, ar an gcaoi seo bíodh an Ghaeilge ar na smaointe is forásaí in Éirinn; is ionann sin agus slánú na Gaeilge. Sí an Ghaeilge athghabháil na hÉireann, sí athghabháil na hÉireann slánú na Gaeilge. Sí teanga na muintire a shlánós an mhuintir.

(Not only should Irish-speakers be participant in this war for the reconquest of Ireland — it is the only thing worth being part of in Ireland — but it is our duty to be its leaders and guides. If Irish is the steering force of the revolution, in this way Irish will be one of the most progressive forces in Ireland: that is the same as reviving Irish. The Irish language is the reconquest of Ireland, and the reconquest of Ireland is the Irish language. The language of the people shall revive the people.)

As with every other aspect of struggle, having agreed on our objectives the rest is a matter of agreeing on how to get there. This may take such small forms as deciding never again to say 'cheerio' and always say 'slán', or it may mean a total involvement in supporting the demands of the language struggle and the demands of the people of the Gaeltachtaí by working actively alongside them.

The media demand special attention because of their importance in influencing their audiences' opinions and values. In both the 26 and 6 counties Sinn Féin calls for substantial increases in television and radio programmes in the Irish language, with special emphasis on children's programmes, and we have as a long-term aim the establishment of a 32 county television and radio service entirely in Irish.

Our councillors use their elected positions in both the 26 and 6 counties to promote Irish culture in such areas as the erection of street signs in Irish, grant aid for feiseanna, bilingual council stationery and signs, the use of Irish at formal council occasions, and an emphasis on Irish music and dances at council-sponsored social events. We also want to see councils in the 26 counties supporting organisations engaged in promoting the Irish language, such as Conradh na Gaeilge, Comhaltas Ceolteoirí Éireann and Cumann Lúthchleas Gael.

In relation to the Gaeltachtaí we recognise that the inferior social and economic infrastructure must be remedied if these strongholds of the language are to grow or even to avoid extinction. Hospital care is a major problem, with people having to travel long distances, and there is a special need for hospital units with Irish-speaking staff in each of the Gaeltachtaí. A fully elected Údarás na Gaeltachta should have the powers of a county council and full control of all planning in the area. They should set up a land bank and prevent land being bought over by companies and individuals which will not promote the interests of the Gaeltacht.

A vital role in the cultural revival has been played by the prisoners in the prisons and concentration camps of the 6 counties, but they are denied the right to receive publications or letters in Irish or to speak Irish during visits; they are forbidden even to wear the Fáinne, to play Gaelic football or to have Irish musical instruments such as the bodhrán and tin whistle. Sinn Féin campaigns for the removal of those bans and for the prisoners' right to study Irish at formal classes up to degree level.

What is crucial is an understanding that the Irish language is the reconquest of Ireland and the reconquest of Ireland is the Irish language. A failure to grasp this, apart from a legitimate patriotic desire to restore our own language and maintain a separate Irish cultural identity, means that, as a dustbin of Anglo-American culture, we will be morally, psychologically, intellectually and materially worse off.

Sinn Féin Today

> My business is revolution.
>
> *James Connolly*

SINN FÉIN IS the only political organisation in Ireland which is substantially organised and active on a 32 county basis. Despite the censorship of Section 31 of the Broadcasting Act, the combined campaigns of harassment and black propaganda by the Dublin and London governments and our own organisational weaknesses, Sinn Féin is a growing force in Irish politics. That this is so is not only a tribute to our members and supporters but is also proof of the validity of our political position and of the relevancy of our policies.

I am quite certain that none of the establishment parties could survive as we have if they had to function in similar conditions. Until 1974 Sinn Féin was banned under British law in the 6 counties and although the late Maire Drumm and others provided a public leadership during this period Sinn Fein lacked the organisation for active political interventions and was primarily underground and thus functioning in a restricted way. While the lifting of the ban means that Sinn Féin membership is no longer an indictable offence we continue to be subjected to a wide range of repressive legislation and petty harassment in both parts of this island.

This harassment takes many forms, from constant interference with well-known activists to intimidation of new members. In the 26 counties especially the targetting of new members by the Special Branch is a long-established police practice. Special Branch officers visit the homes and workplaces — if they are fortunate enough to be in work — of new recruits, especially young ones, and question parents and employers about the political activities of their offspring or employees. Pubs and hotels which rent or lend rooms for meetings often receive similar visits and enquiries about the licenses. Indeed, Coalition's Gaeltacht Minister Paddy O'Toole's intimidation of the Irish-speaking community at Rath Carn is a recent example of political interference in order to prevent Sinn Féin from renting conference facilities. Our members in the 6 counties are frequently victims of assassination by loyalist and British terror gangs, and of all the political parties Sinn Féin has suffered most in this regard.

Recruitment to Sinn Féin used to occur primarily in the wake of events such as the 1969 pogroms, internment, Bloody Sunday and the hunger strikes, so that many people became absorbed into Sinn Féin but not educated into it. Thus there was a lack of unified political consciousness and in the absence of a relevant political education process there was no planned development of republican politics. This vacuum was, of course, filled by other political groupings and it assisted, for example, the growth of the SDLP just as the same kind of lack had contributed to the growth of Fianna Fáil decades earlier. It also led to a certain ignoring of the need for political struggle in the 26 counties.

In the 6 counties, while Sinn Féin was more heavily involved with nationalist communities, few structured and thus durable links were forged from this relationship and no real advances were made. Sinn Féin was by and large perceived, and was in reality, a poor second cousin to the IRA. This was not only how we were seen by supporters and opponents; in many ways it was also how we viewed ourselves.

Much of the change in this situation has come about because of the length of the struggle, for the struggle itself has politicised republicans. So, while there is still a spontaneous move towards Sinn Féin in the wake of some specific action like a British attack on a republican funeral, there is also, as Sinn Féin becomes more relevant on a whole range of issues and more competent on the national question, a steady and consistent flow of recruits into our ranks. New members, especially young people who have lived their entire lives in the struggle, are of a developed political calibre. They have been politicised because the political situation has been continuously developing and because the crisis has been going on for so long.

While spontaneity may be regarded as an element in the political weakness of organised republicanism, in many ways when properly harnessed it is also one of its greatest strengths, making it a living movement in struggle. Republicanism is a very potent force in Irish politics but the vehicle of organised republicanism is still weak organisationally and our underdevelopment in this respect is something which we recognise and which we are constantly addressing.

Electoral success in the 6 counties and in specific areas in the 26 has accelerated this process of developing a party political organisation. There is nothing which concentrates the mind of a political party as much as an electoral campaign and while we do not restrict ourselves to electoralism — indeed we see it merely as one facet in a many-faceted struggle of campaigns, street agitation, cultural resistance, publicity work and education — our electoral successes have played a major role in changing the nature of Sinn Féin.

For example, prior to the 1985 local elections in the 6 counties we had no party whip and were providing no consistent, organised focus for the few local councillors that we had in the 26 counties. Suddenly we found ourselves with about 100 councillors in the 32 counties, some of them in majority positions, with two of them actually in the chair of district councils in the 6 counties. While this had occurred previously in the 26 counties it had done so with much less public or media attention. Now we had very rapidly to apply ourselves to developing ways to service our councillors, to work out a method of accountability, to create the machinery for them to come together to discuss common problems, at the same time making sure that these elected representatives would not become divorced from the grass roots of the party. Recognising the reality of the 6 counties as an electoral unit, we now have a 6 County Executive of Sinn Féin and we have a national chairperson with responsibility for party discipline — in effect, a party whip.

Our electoral intervention has exploded the myth that the republican movement enjoyed no support and it has extended our relationships with our constituents. We can now get certain things done and we have access to the departments of the establishment bureaucracy that are relevant to people's everyday problems and needs.

The electoral intervention has helped to develop the party and to get rid of the novelty of politics for many of our members. There was a great feeling of euphoria after the Assembly election results. From euphoria we went into contesting other elections — we fought ten in four years (more than any other party because we are organised in both parts of Ireland) — and we began to develop a very committed bunch of political workers. The activists had to think; they had to apply themselves to problems, issues, structures and aspects of struggle which they had never really had to consider before. In the process of our campaign everything was done and said by the Irish and British establishments to make it difficult for the electorate to vote for us, the London government going to great lengths to try to deprive many of our supporters of their votes; yet despite all the pressures that were brought to bear the people did vote for us, to the extent that in Belfast, the informal capital city of the 6 counties, Sinn Féin has become the majority nationalist party.

I find this fact particularly satisfying not only because of the stark contrast with the situation when I joined Sinn Féin but also because of Belfast's historical ties with the conception of Irish republicanism in the 1790s. Republicanism is alive and well once more in Belfast city, the political bastion of Unionism and sectarianism; republican politics and methods of struggle are debated there today as eagerly as they were in the days of Tone, Hope and Henry Joy. And no amount of manipulation or pretending it is otherwise by our opponents can disguise this fact.

In Dublin, also, in the last few years Sinn Féin has gained significant support in the working class areas. While this support is coming from those who are most disadvantaged by society, at the same time we have made it clear that we seek to contest some of the areas of support which are currently enjoyed by the Labour Party, Fianna Fáil and the Workers' Party. We seek to build support among the employed and the organised working class and the small business people. In rural areas our natural constituency lies with the working farmers, small business people and rural working class. This section of people have consistently and instinctively remained anti-imperialist and pro-republican in their outlook and there is a potential for us to convert their latent support for the reconquest of Ireland into active support for Sinn Féin.

In order to realise our potential we have to develop our organisation very considerably and we have to move into the mainstream of political relevancy. A problem we experience is that many republicans have long had a compartmentalised attitude to their republican activities whereby they pursue republican 'politics' in isolation from their involvement in community groups, trade unions, co-operative or tenant organisations. We are seeking to change that, to break down self-isolation and to develop policy and strategy that will encourage our members to work in their trade unions and other organisations as republicans.

However, we are aware of precedents in this area which we wish to avoid; we are aware in particular of the record of the Workers' Party, with their secret cumainn, their penchant for manipulation and their generally opportunistic approach to work in the trade unions. It is a record which reinforces for us the importance of acting in an open, non-opportunistic and declared fashion in whatever organisations or campaigns we are engaged in. At all times republicans need to proceed at the level of people's understanding, winning support from that perspective, working alongside people and sharing in their struggles, never getting too far ahead and never getting removed from the activity of the situation.

The organisations of 'Concerned Parents' in Dublin offer a good example of republicans working well in this fashion. The local communities have organised themselves against drugs and drug pushers, and local republicans as members of these communities were, and remain, actively involved. Of course, the republicans could have intervened independently — armed IRA interventions against the main drug suppliers or pushers would undoubtedly have enjoyed widespread support in areas blighted by drugs — but the militant actions of the Concerned Parents, the community ostracisation of the pushers, and the humane community attitudes towards drug addicts have had a more lasting and deeper effect, not just on the issue of drug addiction among Dublin's youth but also in instilling a consciousness of their own power in working-class communities.

The Gaelic revival in the 6 counties has proceeded in much the same fashion, and in other areas of work, though with less dramatic results and with less publicity, Sinn Féin is developing along similar lines. We have come a long way from being largely a protest movement built around the objective of an end to British rule and in opposition to the more obvious aspects of British rule. We have developed into a party which has a potential for support in the 26 counties; this potential has been exaggerated by the establishment — indeed some Coalition Ministers are paranoid about us (suffering perhaps from guilty memories of the past) — but the potential exists nonetheless.

In the 6 counties our support base is well established by recent election results and far from being the criminal thugs, psychopaths and isolated terrorists of British propaganda Sinn Féin is established in a bedrock of support in nationalist areas; the SDLP can no longer claim to be the sole representatives of nationalist opinion. In this regard the emergence of Sinn Féin may have unnecessarily brought out some of the class differences between ourselves and the SDLP leadership. These differences are there, of course, indeed they are dictated by the class nature of the struggle and they should not be disguised, but it might have been better in this phase of the independence struggle if there could have been some kind of general unity, in which both parties would agree to disagree on social and economic issues and maximise pressure on points of agreement. Whether this is feasible or not is impossible to say without dialogue; perhaps there is little on which we could have agreed.

The SDLP, as a partitionist party seeking a reformed 6 county arrangement, has consistently refused to examine the potential for pan-nationalist unity even on a limited basis. Invitations from Sinn Féin have been rejected by the SDLP leadership, often in the most condescending and insulting fashion. One of the things I have discovered about career politicians is that, Sinn Féin being a largely working class party, the politically organised middle class cannot cope with what they see as the audacity of people like ourselves thinking we can do things that they were put through college and university to do.

They were taught their politics, methods of management, public relations work and other skills by experts. We learned ours on the streets, in prison and through a process of self-education. Working class people denied the opportunity, in most cases, of advanced formal education have coped tremendously with all the problems of creating and maintaining an active political movement — not merely a political party which emerges before and retires after elections but a movement in perpetual struggle. After sixteen years of upheaval I feel that it is an achievement in itself to have the type of support we do have, especially considering the opposition we face.

The way in which we work within Sinn Féin is different to the way in which any of the other parties work. We have encouraged an openess in the party in which in a frank but comradely fashion all issues are discussed. No subject is taboo. Our leadership actually encourages constructive criticism of itself, regular re-examination of our strategies and reviews of our policies. This is not to suggest that we are perfect; far from it. We suffer from all the weaknesses of human nature, but by understanding the necessity for revolutionary leadership and having grasped that this involves all of our membership we have made considerable advances in the development of a collective leadership.

You cannot take a vote on every single thing that comes up but I think that other political leaderships expect their members to accept that their leadership should be permitted to do their thinking for them. In Sinn Féin we are striving for a situation where our membership participates in the decision-making process in the fullest way possible and to the fullest extent. They then understand and support these decisions because they have been involved in the decision-making and thus they will be more committed and capable of implementing these decisions. This is an essential ingredient in the building of a revolutionary party. It also ensures that the right decisions are more likely to be taken.

Of importance also is a willingness to recognise, to admit and to rectify mistakes. Communication is vital and frank and open dialogue between all levels of our organisation is something we are working to create. We all have feet of clay and no revolutionary leadership can be unmindful of this very human condition. Many incompetent people pushed into leadership or seeking leadership because of a desire for power (something I can understand in any context other than the republican movement) have possessed leadership qualities without the other necessary attributes and have thus been absolutely incapable of accepting criticism.

The cult of personality which exists in Irish public life is something which has to be overcome. As Connolly put it,

> In Ireland . . . we have ever seized upon mediocrities
> and made them leaders; invested them in our minds

with all the qualities we idealised, and then when we discovered that our leaders were not heroes but only common mortals, mediocrities, we abused them, or killed them for failing to be better than God made them. Their failure dragged us down along with them because we had insisted that they were wiser than we were, and had stoned whoever declared them to be mere mortals and not all-wise geniuses. Our real geniuses and inspired apostles we never recognised, nor did we honour them. We killed them by neglect, or stoned them whilst they lived, and then went in reverent procession to their graves when they were killed.

Connolly and other writers attribute this tendency to 800 years of British colonial oppression. It is something which must be overcome especially and first of all within the ranks of those seeking to end British colonialism.

The electoral situation in the 26 counties is very different from that in the 6 counties and we suffer from major organisational difficulties. We have to cope with the age-old question of what part reformism plays in the building of support and we are still constructing the foundations for an effective political party in that area. While republicans are very disciplined in terms of loyalty to the movement, we experience a lack of political acumen, which may have to do with our conspiratorial past and which certainly has to do with the confining of the struggle to the 6 counties.

The effects of Section 31 of the Broadcasting Act pose a considerable problem: not so much in terms of support for Sinn Féin specifically but in terms of disinformation — disinformation not just about the British presence in the 6 counties but also in terms of society in the 26 counties. More importantly it denies people their right to freedom of information. The whole ethos that flows from that censorship is very pervasive and results in a failure to investigate issues fully. It is closely related to a mood of revisionism and of turning backs even on the origins of the state. The 26 counties must be unique as a state in that it did nothing to mark the seventieth anniversary of the proclamation of the republic, whereas in any other country such an anniversary would have been marked by pageantry and celebration. The establishment are so afraid of all the skeletons in the cupboards of the state, afraid that if they scratch a Terence MacSwiney up jumps a Bobby Sands, or if — as Dick Spring discovered — they scratch Roger Casement, up jumps Martin Ferris.

The context of censorship in the 26 counties disinforms people and makes life more difficult for us politically. However, Sinn Féin's major problem is our failure to date to build an effective organisation after long periods of self-imposed isolation derived from conspiratorial politics as well as censorship, of harrassment by the guards, and of a lack of political understanding. The only way I know in which this problem can be tackled is by discussing and addressing every single issue which is pertinent. If I have learned anything I have learned that you can only proceed on the basis of people's support, and that you can only enjoy that support if you are approaching people at a level and on ground which they understand. You have to find a common denominator between what you want to do and what people feel needs to be done. Sinn Féin became irrelevant to many people in the 26 counties because republicans failed to examine the society in which they lived and failed to offer a political way forward. Nevertheless, in all the different walks of Irish life there is a grudging respect for the concept of republicanism. As Conor Cruise O'Brien has pointed out, republicanism is in a sense the conscience of the Irish people. There is a feeling that if the Rising of 1916 was, as his generation was taught, right, then the resistance in 1969 was right and in 1986 is right as well. There is a tolerance and an ambivalence because in the back of people's minds is the notion that there is some logic and rectitude to what republicans are saying.

Although Sinn Féin is a 32-county organisation it has been as subject to the uneven development of the two statelets as any other aspect of life on the island, and one way in which this unevenness expresses itself is in terms of a problem of public leadership. The organisation in the 26 counties is in a relatively retarded position and lacks its own identifiable leadership. There are many very able people in the membership and in local leadership positions who are not publicly identifiable outside of their own areas. There are members with plenty of ability, talent and commitment who nevertheless would not be known outside of a Sinn Féin Árd Fheis and who might not even be known by most other Sinn Féin members. And this is a problem which has a special importance in terms of our ability to field and develop candidates for local elections.

In the last 26 county local elections we received a realistic vote which can easily be related to those places where we are well organised and have prominent individuals. We got the vote we deserved. But none of the local election seats won would work out in a general election as a Leinster House seat. The electoral intervention of the H-Block/Armagh Committee at the time of the hunger strike showed an ability to bring out more than the normal republican vote. When, however, shortly after that an electoral intervention was made in the absence of a hunger strike, the figures had shrunk back to the republican vote, at about 5 per cent. This was absolutely predictable. Electoral interventions are successful only in very special conditions. To build and consolidate electoral support a consistent electoral strategy is required. In the hunger strike election voters set aside the very pressing economic priorities and saddled themselves with a hung parliament, and that was significant. But once the hunger strike was over the economic issues came to the fore again and people went back to voting for some kind of stability.

Our electoral experiences provoked a sporadic debate about abstentionism. There was some opposition within Sinn Féin to our electoral strategy because once on the electoral road, if one was serious, one would have to confront the issue of abstentionism.

There is a substantial difference between abstentionism in the 6 counties and in the 26 counties. A large part of the nationalist and republican population in the 6 counties regards abstentionism as posing no problem in terms of giving their votes, because they do not see participation in the institutions of the state as having anything to offer them. But in the 26 counties, while people may be very scornful of the performance of the politicians and cynical about the institutions of the state they nevertheless expect the people they elect to represent them in these institutions. In the 6 counties people can go to an active-abstentionist representative who will work on their behalf in constituency matters. In the 26 counties although a number of Sinn Féin TDs were elected in the 1950s there was never a policy of *active*-abstentionism; if there had been abstentionism might not now be as significant a factor in the organisation.

At the time of writing the debate continues: at the 1984 Sinn Féin Árd Fheis the position was that the issue could not even be debated, but this was changed and the subject was opened up for debate at the 1985 Árd Fheis. Despite its great emotional potential within the movement it was argued in a logical, informative and interesting manner; there was some emotionalism and there were spontaneous outbursts of applause for rhetoric, but in the end, as has often been my experience, the vote was not in accord with the applause and was, in fact, very close. The debate took place without a lead from the platform: it was felt by the Árd Chomhairle at that time to be such a historically divisive issue that the people on the platform should have a free vote and that it would be better to arrive at positions after listening to the debate by the membership rather than having a situation where people might be swayed by the oratory of Martin McGuinness, Danny Morrison, Gerry Adams, or other leading figures.

That situation has now changed. The 1986 Árd Fheis considered an Árd Chomhairle motion calling for an end to our abstentionist attitude to Leinster House. As this book went to press shortly before the Árd Fheis it remained to be seen at the time of writing whether the motion would receive the necessary two-thirds majority. What was clear, however, from the mood in the party, was that abstentionism in regard to Leinster House is going to go. The only question is when. What is certain is that when that happens it will usher in a new era of republican politics and a new dimension to politics in the 26 counties.

There are no real parallels between our current debate and the debate associated with the split in the republican movement in 1970 which led to the creation of the 'Stickies', now the Workers' Party. At that time the IRA leadership had decided to abandon armed struggle and then decided to drop abstentionism. The leadership brought in all its organisers and conducted an intensive indoctrination course, setting the movement on the path of constitutionality. The development can be clearly traced through the speeches and policy changes of the time — the movement from opposition to Stormont to full support for it, from shooting at the RUC to full support for them, from a call for British withdrawal to support for the British presence, from opposition to the EEC to full support. They changed their basic positions in a major ideological somersault and were involved in a new departure.

We are not engaged in any new departure. We are committed absolutely to the objective of Irish independence. And we have no illusions about Leinster House. I share and I understand the republican memory of how Leinster House was imposed on us by summary executions at Ballyseedy and other lonely spots and by the hangman's noose and firing squads in Free State prisons.

To understand the significance of this recent development within Sinn Féin one must understand that it comes after many decades of stagnation. In the past the republican movement was a separatist movement with radical tendencies. In its current embodiment the radical tendency is for the first time in control, and in institutionalising the radical tendency a very important, historic job has been done. In our thinking we have brought to light elements which were obscured in the past. The philosophers and thinkers of the 1916 Rising did not survive it, and this set the stage for counter-revolution. What we have done is that we have taken a step towards reversing the effects of the counter-revolution.

The counter-revolution of that time was followed by the abandonment by the republicans of politics in the context of a monopoly of politics by the establishment, and republicans from then on simply kept harking back. It may have been sufficient in 1918 or 1920 to merely say 'we want the 1916 Proclamation'; but with the growth of the partitionist state, which was functioning effectively, it was no longer adequate and by the '30s it was less and less so.

If we have done nothing else of significance in the 1970s and '80s we have tried to do what was done in the previous high periods of republicanism. The republicans who penned the 1916 Proclamation, who wrote *The Sovereign People* and *Labour in Irish History,* sat down, discussed, thrashed out and developed their politics. They did not simply take what Wolfe Tone had said; they took the principles and they added to them and tried to develop from that basis. No matter how inadequately, we have tried to do the same thing against the background of an absence of significant critical evaluation and reassessment for about sixty years.

We have tried first of all to take the general principles of republicanism as subscribed to in the Proclamation and we have tried under very difficult circumstances to make these relevant. The power and strength of the establishment is massive compared to a collection of working class people such as make up the republican movement. We have tried to make the principles relevant in major ways and in what may be small, mundane ways which are reflected in how we, as opposed to the establishment parties, deal in an electoral sense with a constituent or in a broader sense with someone we are trying to win over.

To take just one example of how we have tried to implement the basic principles in practice: we have decided internally that because of the discrimination against women in Irish society we will have a policy of positive discrimination. The republican movement is not a set of abstract ideas, it is a movement of people in society and it reflects tendencies in society in general. The fact that women have historically not enjoyed a significant role in deciding policy in the movement can be related to the status of women in society as a whole. Nevertheless, the republican movement has probably had a rather better attitude to women than many institutions. There have been many leading republican women and recognition has always been given to the fact that women provided the backbone of the conspiratorial aspect of the movement.

Now we are the only party in Ireland that has by right a quarter of the places on our Árd Chomhairle reserved for women. We have also taken measures to overcome and avoid typecasting or stereotyping of women within the party. While we have a long way to go before women comrades have full equality in Sinn Féin rather than saying that in post-colonial Ireland women will have equality, we have taken small practical steps now, and these are measures which are more telling and more relevant than any noble aspirations.

While we still do not have nearly enough women candidates, women are now certainly playing a fuller role within the organisation. In this context women have started articulating their own demands and the credit for this lies with the women themselves. It is a continuing process involving conflicting views, and it doesn't by any means confine itself to women intervening on 'women's issues'. Seven of Sinn Féin's thirteen national departments are headed by women and the editor of *An Phoblacht* is a woman.

In other aspects of our philosophy and of the development of our organisation we have tried to do the same kind of thing. We hold regular internal conferences at every level of the party and while this may not in itself be very significant they differ radically from party conferences/Árd Fheiseanna in other parties. The Fianna Fáil Árd Fheis, for example, is by and large a jamboree. This serves a useful political purpose but it means that the Árd Fheis is not the place where debate takes place or where policy is formulated and agreed upon. Fine Gael suffers from the same syndrome. In the micro-groups conferences are dominated by doctrinaire lines, splinters, splits and factions.

The Sinn Féin Árd Fheis is a developing phenomenon which perhaps ten years ago was to some extent a jamboree where people came together — there was a social element to it, there was a publicity element, all the obvious advantages of being able to present the public spectacle of a party political conference. There was, however, no meaningful debate on issues other than the obvious. But in the late '70s things began to change and today they are continuing to change.

Our Árd Fheis in 1985 had 249 motions — the largest number ever — on a wide variety of issues. It is actually impossible to deal with as many motions in the hours available and it is inevitable that some interest groups putting forward motions have to experience the frustration of not being able to put their motion and have it discussed. And this is a real problem because one can see that as Sinn Féin becomes involved in more and more issues and as republicans develop their consciousness about the depth of the struggle they naturally feel the need to put forward their particular strategies or tactics.

This process of critical self-analysis and reappraisal has led to frank and open discussion on many issues which would not otherwise have surfaced. The end result is that we have an Árd Fheis which is unique but which presents difficulties in public presentation; an Árd Fheis which discusses a whole spectrum of issues from travellers' rights to incest (an issue which no other political party to my knowledge has ever discussed) and AIDS.

These, I know, are minority interest subjects but they are important nonetheless and they show that the Árd Fheis is not just being used as a jamboree but that it is actually an open democratic forum in which members dictate policy and avail of the opportunity to win support for their positions.

Another example of the realisation of the importance of republican politics leading to a structured approach can be found in the production and availability of republican literature. A wide range of this literature (our opponents call it propaganda) is produced and distributed by Republican Publications and as we have improved our political structures and our political understanding the quality of this literature has improved.

Educational pamphlets, a number of small books, collections of poetry, policy documents, posters, an annual calendar and a republican diary are but some of the items produced and distributed by a small group of voluntary workers. They started with little previous experience and only a few hundred pounds but with lots of common sense and commitment they have established a thoroughly professional operation. Before this structured approach the production of republican literature was sporadic — indeed it may have amounted only to a handful of pamphlets in as many years. Now at least one new publication on some aspect of our struggle is produced every few months.

An Phoblacht, which merged with *Republican News* in 1979, is a radical weekly in as full a sense as one would wish; it can be improved, of course, but its weekly production as a centralised expression and platform of republican politics is a great achievement. If one looks at past issues of either of the two papers before the merger and seeks to analyse them as representing the politics of the movement one may very well come to inadequate conclusions. At times, especially when many republicans were underground and unconcerned or unable to influence the content or the presentation of our newspapers, they were really a reflection of the particular politics and emphases of the few people who worked very hard to produce them. Since the merger and our re-orientation this has changed and *An Phoblacht* has gone from strength to strength, praised even by our critics as the best political newspaper in Ireland today.

Sinn Féin also produces a large amount of bilingual material. Indeed *Nuacht Feirste* is one of only three Irish language newspapers published in Ireland, and *Saoirse,* our Irish language magazine, is the only political magazine published in Irish. Copies of *IRIS,* an occasional English language production, are now collector's items.

None of this short but slightly boastful section is an attempt to suggest that we have perfected the art of producing revolutionary literature. It is simply an effort to show that having realised the necessity for such literature we proceeded, with some success, to fulfill that need. It is also an unashamed and proudly proclaimed example of the fact that people in struggle can change things and in the changing learn how to improve and perfect their struggle.

There is still a lot of work to be done before the task of building Sinn Féin into the mass organiser of the Irish people is completed. We face an uncertain future but we can at least be confident that we face it with as much determination, more confidence and with more experience than any previous generation of Irish republicans. We know that we survived in the past and consolidated in the present despite all our weaknesses and in spite of the strengths of our opponents. We face the future confident in that knowledge.

Peace in Ireland?

> As to any union between the two islands, believe us when we assert that our union rests upon our mutual independence. We shall love each other if we are left to ourselves. It is the union of mind which ought to bind these nations together.
>
> *United Irishmen*

This book outlines in part a history which is in itself the reason why there is no peace in Ireland. One of the major conclusions to be drawn is that the British government is the major obstacle and the most consistent barrier to peace in Ireland and that a British withdrawal is a necessary pre-condition if we are to secure the basis upon which peace can be built in Ireland. Responsibility, therefore, for the problem created by this government must also be shared by the people who elected it and in whose name it governs part of Ireland.

The people of Britain should be interested in what their government is doing in Ireland and in what their army is doing here. Sadly this interest is only aroused when the problem involves them directly. The issues, closely guarded and distorted by their government, are clouded and deliberately confused. Some individuals involved in the British news media have in fact protested at the lack of objective reporting of the situation in Ireland and the lack of coverage given to those opposed to their government's involvement.

Meanwhile British soldiers and Irish civilians are dying on Irish streets, Irish prisoners have died and are ill-treated in British jails and there have been periodic bombings in England itself. The English people must therefore concede, regardless of the confusions and distortions of facts, that their government has not brought peace to Ireland.

They must decide if responsibility for our long war can be traced to the system of colonial plunder based in England. If they so decide, as an impartial people must, and if they are true democrats they must argue for the withdrawal of their soldiers and for the dismantling of that system. It is their government, 'the Mother of Parliaments', which controls Irish destinies. The government has no rights in Ireland or rights to Ireland. British people should help us to remove it. They should realise that the granting of independence to Ireland must benefit both countries (especially the working class of both countries) equally, because all the reasons for distrust and hatred will be removed and a real and lasting friendship would be created in their place.

Democrats in Britain and throughout the world must insist on peace in Ireland. They can best do this by campaigning for the removal of the cause of the conflict. They can pressurise the British government into withdrawing completely from Ireland. By doing so they will not only rid Ireland of the decadent and mercenary system which divides us and exploits our people. They will also forge an alliance which will guarantee freedom for oppressed people, everywhere.

In Ireland as well there is need for maximum pressure to be exerted on the British government. Part of this book shows clearly how the economic situation, the massive social stresses and the pro-imperialist policies of the Dublin government are linked to the colonial situation in the 6 counties. Both share a common source and a common cause. It is obvious, therefore, that any attempt to remove that source, and thus its effects, must unite the people affected in the struggle to build up an alternative. At national level and on a 32 county basis, this requires mobilisation of all progressive forces and of all those denied political, economic, social or cultural freedom behind the demand for British withdrawal and Irish national self-determination.

It also requires involvement by republicans and anti-imperialists on every front, North and South, in this struggle. Identifying only with sections of the working class and outlining general policy on aspects that affect them is not enough. We need unity against imperialism, against one enemy and in one struggle. This cannot be accomplished solely by the republican movement. It can only be secured by the people themselves. In the 26, as much as the 6 counties, this is a necessity, not only to secure the future success of the present struggle, but to safeguard now the welfare of those repressed by the policies of the Dublin government.

Ireland, to secure and ensure the prosperity of our people,

must win not only political freedom but economic independence as well. This economic independence, coupled with social and cultural freedom, must be in the sense of securing our own control over our own economic surplus so that we can apply it to productive capital investment for the planned economic development of the whole island and of all our people. This means the reconquest of Ireland by the Irish people.

This cannot be done under the present systems. It means national independence and a social revolution in all Ireland. These objectives can only be achieved when ordinary people identify with them. This support can only be achieved nationally when it is worked for at local level. This can only be done by hard work, by example, through dialogue and by linking the local problems where they belong — as part of our British problem and at the door of both partitionist governments.

An object, as Mellows declared, a target, must be presented for the enemy to hit at and the programme for national self-determination must be translated into something definite, providing the people with a rallying point and republicans with a focusing point. The struggle needs therefore to be extended politically onto a 32 county level, and must not be restricted to the 6 counties. We cannot hope to build a 32 county alternative if we do not build a 32 county struggle.

We must place our objectives before the people, we must link together all the threads of our British problem and build people's resistence to it. Republicans are not intent on replacing the present systems with a republican ruling class. We believe in the people themselves as the sovereign authority. We want Ireland for the Irish. We want an Irish democracy in Ireland.

It follows then that we must continually examine our tactics, our strategies and our short-term objectives. We must accept that we are not always in the best position to justify our stand, our philosophy or our activities. We must therefore ensure that our conduct, our attitudes and our discipline, in the face of a powerful and unscrupulous enemy, will encourage, not discourage, continued support for the objectives we strive for.

Finally, we must remain totally opposed to the cult of sectarianism. Sectarianism will only be defeated when its source is removed. The removal of the cause of sectarianism, of the British prop which sustains it, will initiate a coming together of all our people and the undoing of sectarian influences, violence and politics. We want a united people, not merely a single geographical unit. By removing the source of division and bitterness we will ensure the beginning of the process for the transformation of our country.

Such a transformation will not be accomplished by establishment or sectarian party politicians, by establishment figures, by Church leaders, or by British warlords. It can only be achieved by the people who have most to gain from such a transformation. It can ony be achieved by the ordinary people uniting to build a new society in Ireland and a new future for us all.

In this belief I look forward with confidence to the future, hopeful, even if this hope is nurtured amid stress and turmoil, that what I have detailed in these pages will contribute in some small way to a happy outcome for all our people, and to the peaceful and final resolution of our British problem.

Publisher's Note

On 2 November 1986, at its Árd Fheis in the Mansion House, Dublin, Sinn Féin dropped its abstentionist attitude to Leinster House, the Dublin parliament.

In his Presidential address to the Árd Fheis Gerry Adams indicated that 'If we do contest on an attendance ticket, the election after the next one will be the first serious test of our ability to win major support.' He stressed that the aim was to register broad political gains rather than immediate gains in terms of a seat or seats in Leinster House.

Sources

Books

Adams, Gerry: *Falls Memories* (Dingle 1982)

Comerford, Maire: *The First Dáil*

Connolly, James: *Labour and Easter Week* (Dublin 1949)

Connolly, James: *Labour in Ireland* (Dublin 1973)

Connolly, James: *Socialism and Nationalism* (Dubin 1948)

Connolly, James: *The Workers' Republic* (Dublin 1951)

Coughlan, Anthony: *Fooled Again* (Cork 1986)

Cronin, Sean: *Ireland Since the Treaty*

Darby, John (ed.): *Northern Ireland: the Background to the Conflict* (Belfast 1983)

De Fréine, Séan: *The Great Silence* (Cork 1978)

Farrell, Michael: *Arming the Protestants* (Dingle 1983)

Farrell, Michael: *Northern Ireland: The Orange State* (London 1976)

Greaves, C. Desmond: *Liam Mellows and the Irish Revolution* (London 1971)

Greaves, C. Desmond: *The Life and Times of James Connolly* (London 1961)

Kelleher, Derry: *On to the Republic* (Dublin 1982)

McCann, Eamonn: *War and an Irish Town* (London 1974)

Pearse, P.H.: *The Murder Machine* (Mercier 1976)

Pamphlets

Adams, Gerry: *Our British Problem* (unpublished)

Adams, Gerry: *Peace in Ireland*

(European Security Studies No 2): *British's Undefended Frontier*

McMillan, Liam: *Separatist, Socialist, Republican*

Ó Cadhain, Máirtín: *Gluaiseacht na Gaeilge: Gluaiseacht ar Strae*

Ó Cadhain, Máirtín: *Irish Above Politics*

Ó Maolchraoibhe, Padraig, et al: *The Role of the Language in Ireland's Cultural Revival*

Ó Murchú, Eoin: *Culture and the Revolution*

(Sinn Féin): *Ag Foglaim na Gaeilge*

(Sinn Féin Educational Lectures): *Loyalism; Republicanism; Socialism and Nationalism*

Glossary

Arms Trial   In 1970 Neil Blaney and Charles Haughey — both members of the Fianna Fáil Cabinet of Jack Lynch —, Haughey's brother, Captain Kelly — a Free State army intelligence officer —, John Kelly of the IRA, and Albert Luykx — a Belgian businessman —, were charged with illegally importing arms. The defence maintained that the arms importation was sanctioned by the Dublin government; the charges were dismissed.

Ashe, Thomas   Writer, musician, teacher and republican; leader of the IRB after the 1916 Rising in which he commanded a successful action in Co. Meath. In 1917 his death on hunger strike, in pursuit of political satus, rallied mass support for national independence.

Ballyseedy   Scene of one of the worst atrocities of the Civil War, when Free State forces killed several republicans in cold blood.

Bata scóir   A stick marked to record the times a schoolchild spoke Irish; each additional notch incurred a beating.

Black and Tans   Taking their names from their khaki uniforms and black police caps and belts, they were a semi-mercenary force recruited from unemployed ex-servicemen. Notorious for their brutality and indiscipline, they served in Ireland from 1920-22.

Casement, Roger   Knighted in 1911 for his service to the British Crown; joined the Volunteers in 1913 and organised arms for the Rising. Hanged by the British in 1916.

Collins, Michael   Member of the Volunteers in the 1916 Rising; Minister of Home Affairs and later Minister of Finance in the First Dáil, and director of organisation and intelligence for the IRA. One of the signatories of the Anglo-Irish Treaty of 1921 and subsequently Commander-in-Chief of the government forces in the Civil War. Killed in an ambush in 1922.

Connolly, James   Founded the Irish Socialist Republican Party in 1896; in America 1903-10 he worked as an organiser for the Industrial Workers of the World (IWW); Belfast organiser of the Irish Transport and General Workers Union (ITGWU) 1911-13. Involved in the Dublin lock-out of 1913 and in the formation of the Irish Citizen Army, a workers' defence force. He was in the vanguard of the struggle against imperialism and joined with revolutionary nationalists in the 1916 Rising, being one of the signatories of the Proclamation; wounded in the Rising, he was executed by the British authorities.

Craig, William   Minister of Home Affairs in the 6 counties 1963/4; Minister of Health and Local Government 1964; Minister of Development 1965; Minister of Home Affairs again 1966-68. Established the Ulster Vanguard Party in 1972 with strong support from paramilitaries.

Cumman   Local political party branch.

De Valera, Eamon   Commandant in the Irish Volunteers in the 1916 Rising, he was sentenced to death but was reprieved, becoming President of Sinn Féin in 1917 and President of the Dáil in 1919. Opposed the Treaty and was the political leader of the anti-Treaty forces in the Civil War of 1922-23. Founded the Fianna Fáil Party in 1926. Prime Minister 1932-48, 1951-54, 1957-59; President of 26 counties 1959-73.

Drumm, Maire   Acting President of Provisional Sinn Féin 1971-72; Vice-President 1972-76.

Easter Lily   A badge in the form of a lily worn to honour the 1916 Rising.

Fáinne   A ring; a badge worn to denote an Irish speaker.

Faulkner, Brian   Unionist MP for East Down at Stormont 1949-73; Minister of Home Affairs 1959-63, Minister of Commerce 1963-69, Minister of Development 1969-71, Prime Minister 1971-72. Set up breakaway Unionist Party of Northern Ireland in 1974; Chief Executive, Northern Ireland Executive, January-May 1974.

FCA   Fórsa Cosanta Áitiúl, the local defence force of the 26 counties.

Feiseanna, fleadhanna   Festivals of Irish music and dance.

Ferris, Martin   Skipper of the *Marita Anne*.

Gaelic League   Founded 1893, organised Irish lessons and promoted the language, music and games, becoming a major element in the nationalist movement.

Gaeltacht   An Irish speaking area.

Galltacht   English speaking area.

GPO   General Post Office, occupied by the revolutionary forces as the focal point of the 1916 Rising.

Hyde, Douglas   Scholar, professor of modern languages, collector of folklore, poetry and song, translator. First President of the Gaelic League 1893; first Professor of Modern Irish, UCD, 1909; Free State Senator 1925-26; First President of 26 counties 1937-45.

Irish Republican Brotherhood (IRB)   A revolutionary secret society dedicated to establishing an Irish Republic by force; it was first known as the Fenians and organised a rising in 1867. It was re-organised as the IRB in 1873, planned the 1916 Rising and re-organised the Volunteers into the IRA in 1918-19. Under Michael Collins's influence it supported the Treaty, and ceased to have much influence after his death.

Kitson, General Frank   Served in Kenya, Malaya and Cyprus before commanding the 39th Infantry Brigade in the 6 counties, 1970-72. Developed British army strategy of psychological warfare and counter subversion. Author of *Low-Intensity Operations*.

Lalor, James Fintan   Fighter in the cause of agrarian reform, Lalor later edited the *Irish Felon*, newspaper of the Young Irelanders.

Larkin, James   Great syndicalist and agitator, founder of the Irish Transport and General Workers Union (ITGWU) and leader of the Dublin workers in the 1913 lock-out. His absence and later imprisonment in America removed him from the scene of Irish working-class politics at a crucial stage and after his return in 1923 he was never again the same towering force.

Lemass, Sean   Member of the Volunteers in the 1916 Rising; founder member of Fanna Fáil; Minister for Industry and Commerce 1932-39, 1941-48, 1951-54, 1957-59, Minister for Supplies 1939-45; Deputy Prime Minister 1945-48, 1951-54, 1957-59; Prime Minister 1959-66.

MacDonagh, Thomas   Poet and teacher, he helped found Pearse's bilingual school in 1908. Member of IRB military council set up to plan the Rising; signed the 1916 Proclamation and was executed on 3 May 1916.

MacSwiney, Terence   Author of plays, poetry and political journalism and of *Principals of Freedom*; full-time organiser for the Irish Volunteers. Elected to first Dáil for West Cork; elected Lord Mayor of Cork; arrested in Cork City Hall in 1920, his subsequent hunger strike focussed world attention on Ireland; he died on the 74th day of his hunger strike in Brixton Prison.

'Marita Anne'   A fishing trawler with arms bound for the IRA which was captured near Fenit in County Kerry in 1985, near the spot where Roger Casement had been captured by British forces in 1916 following the failed attempt to land arms for the Volunteers from the *Aud*. The capture of the *Marita Anne* coincided with the unveiling of a monument to Roger Casement by Dick Spring, leader of the Labour Party and Deputy Prime Minister.

Mellows, Liam   Leader of the Galway Volunteers in the 1916 Rising and a member of the First Dáil, he was shot without trial while a prisoner of the Free State forces in 1922.

NICRA   Northern Ireland Civil Rights Association. Set up in January 1967 it spearheaded the early years of the civil rights campaign.

O'Malley, Ernie   A writer and republican, he fought in the 1916 Rising and with the republicans in the Civil War. His two celebrated books are *On Another Man's Wound* and *The Singing Flame*.

O'Neill, Terence   6 County Minister for Finance 1956-63; Prime Minister 1963-69.

Orange Order   Founded in 1795 during Protestant-Catholic clashes over land, it was dedicated to maintaining Protestant supremacy and the link with Britain. No Catholic and no-one whose close relatives are Catholic may be a member. It played an important part in defeating Home Rule; after partition the Unionist Party developed from the Order, while the 'B' Specials were almost exclusively Orangemen. As well as being effective in mobilising the Protestant masses, it has had close links with the British Conservative Party.

Paisley, Ian (Rev.)   Loyalist demagogue who, in 1951, set up a 'Free Prebyterian Church'; from this base he attacked the civil rights campaign, the so-called 'Romeward trend' of the Prebyterian Church and the 'treachery' of Unionist leaders who met with 26 county politicians. MP for North Antrim since 1970, he founded the Democratic Unionist Party in 1971.

Pearse, Patrick   Educationalist, writer and revolutionary; founder of a bilingual school and a member of the Irish Republican Brotherhood (IRB), he was Commander-in-Chief of the forces of the Irish Republic in the 1916 Rising; one of the signatories of the Proclamation, he was President of the Provisional Government and was executed by the British.

Republican Congress   Initiated by Peadar O'Donnell, George Gilmore and Michael Price, the Republican Congress of 1934 was an attempt to unite republicans, socialists and trade unionists in an anti-imperialist front. Many later fought with the International Brigade in Spain.

RUC   Royal Ulster Constabulary. The 6 county police force.

Sellafield British nuclear power station in Cumbria responsible for dumping radioactive waste in the Irish Sea.

Shoneen Seoinín: toady.

Slógadh Gathering.

Twelfth of July Annual demonstrations to celebrate the victory of King William of Orange over the Catholic King James at the battle of the Boyne in 1690.

UDA Ulster Defence Association. The largest Protestant paramilitary organisation.

UDR Ulster Defence Regiment. A part-time reserve force, its membership drawn initially from disbanded 'B' Specials.

UVF Ulster Volunteer Force (1913-23): founded in 1913 as a private army to resist Home Rule and armed with 25,000 German rifles; many members of the UVF enlisted in the British army and served in the First World War in a separate unit, the 36th (Ulster) Division. In the 1920s the UVF were involved in pogroms and other attacks on Catholics.

Ulster Volunteer Force (1966-present): The name was revived in 1966 by a loyalist sectarian paramilitary group who murdered two Catholics in that year and later planted the bombs that led to the fall of O'Neill in 1969. It remains in existence as a loyalist paramilitary organisation.